MW00640434

THE
DOCTRINE OF
SPIRITUAL
PERFECTION

THE DOCTRINE OF SPIRITUAL PERFECTION

Anselm Stolz, O.S.B.

Translated by
Aidan Williams, O.S.B.

Introduction by
Stephen Fields, S.J.

A Herder & Herder Book
The Crossroad Publishing Company
New York

The Crossroad Publishing Company
481 Eighth Avenue, New York, NY 10001

Originally published under the title *Theologie der Mystik*
© 1936 Friedrich Pustet, Regensberg, Germany
English translation copyright © 1938 by Herder & Herder
Introduction to the 2001 Edition copyright © 2001 by
The Crossroad Publishing Company

All rights reserved. No part of this book may be
reproduced, stored in a retrieval system, or transmitted, in
any form or by any means, electronic, mechanical,
photocopying, recording, or otherwise, without the written
permission of The Crossroad Publishing Company.

Nihil obstat: D. Justinus McCann O.S.B.
Censor Congregat. Angliae O.S.B.

Imprimatur: RR.DD. Edmundus Kelly O.S.B., Abbas Praeses

Nihil obstat: F.J. Holweck, Censor Librorum

Imprimatur: Joannes J. Glennon, Archiepiscopus

August 10, 1938

Printed in the United States of America

Library of Congress Catalog Card Number: 00-110813

ISBN: 0-8245-1887-X

INTRODUCTION
TO THE 2001 EDITION

A new edition of Anselm Stolz's lucid treatise on the mystical life is especially timely. As a German Benedictine who taught at the Anselmo in Rome, Stolz (1900-1942) brings to bear on the subject two movements in Catholic thought then in full flower. He combines the renewed interest in the thought St. Thomas Aquinas begun by Leo XIII's 1879 encyclical *Aeterni Patris* with the so-called 'new theology,' a return to the biblical and patristic sources of Christian thought. His approach to the spiritual life thus seeks to counterbalance the dominance of psychology and phenomenology which, even in Catholic circles, have led to distortion. These two disciplines assume that extraordinary phenomena—voices, visions, ecstasies, and stigmata—are essential to mysticism. By contrast, Stolz seeks to integrate the mystical life into the central dogmas of the Catholic faith and thus to recover it as the perfection of grace available to *all* Christians. Hence the suitability of the translator's choice of English title of a work originally published in German as *Theologie der Mystik*. Since mysticism is the flowering of the virtues and gifts of the Spirit implanted by the sacraments and nurtured in prayer, a proper understanding of it provides a paradigm for understanding the nature and goal of every Christian's inner life. Stolz does not accept the strong distinction between mysticism and the usual modes of Christian prayer. Developing a balanced reciprocity between these, he locates their common essence in the human person's being created in the image and likeness of God.

So pervasive is the influence of psychology on the analysis of mysticism that Stolz's approach may strike the modern reader as eccentric or anachronistic. Much of this psychological influence actually has a recent provenance in Christianity, which Stolz traces to the Spanish mystics of the 16th century, especially the Carmelites Teresa of Ávila and John of the Cross. Although respectful of the contributions of these Church doctors, he sees in their efforts to delineate precise stages in the experiential knowledge of God the seeds of a reductionism. One might well argue that these have germinated fully since being cultivated by William James and Evelyn Underhill at the turn of the twentieth century. Despite the remarkable achievements of these scholars who, together with Baron Friedrich von Hügel, were largely responsible for reviving contemporary interest in the field, they have also contributed to its dislocation from the systematic explication of the Christian faith.[1] In the *Varieties of Religious Experience*, James treats

---

[1] Friedrich von Hügel, *The Mystical Element of Religion as Studied in Saint Catherine of Genoa and Her Friends* (New York: Crossroad, 1999); originally published in 1908.

mystical experiences as isolated and extraordinary psychological phenomena. As defying adequate articulation, they temporarily render their recipient passive while conveying a knowledge that challenges the normal categories of understanding and perceiving reality. Mystics thus become bizarre cases for disinterested study: Their social utility must be justified, and their claims to know the divine, though perhaps authoritative for themselves, cannot be compelling to those who have not shared similar experiences.[2] In *Mysticism*, Evelyn Underhill corrects James's view of mystical experiences as discreet phenomena by situating them within an organic pattern of human development. But like James, her method is both phenomenological and psychological. She surveys an impressive range of mystical writings, Christian and other, and then seeks an explanation for the experiences they evince in a general theory of consciousness.[3]

Stolz contends that nothing could be more alien to the main lines of the Christian theology of mysticism. In an effort to ground the phenomenon's psychological aspects dogmatically, he returns to St. Paul's second letter to the Corinthians, the Greek fathers, and Thomas Aquinas. By synthesizing these biblical, patristic, and scholastic sources, Stolz discovers a basic definition. "Mysticism," he says, "is the experience of that process of being drawn into the stream of divine life, a process which is accomplished in the

[2] William James, *The Varieties of Religious Experience* (New York: MacMillan, 1997) lectures 16-17; originally the Gifford Lectures at Edinburgh 1901-02.

[3] Evelyn Underhill, *Mysticism: The Nature and Development of Spiritual Consciousness* (England: Oneworld Publications, 1999) especially Part Two; originally published in 1911.

sacraments." (234) By explaining the key terms of this definition, he proceeds to develop his theology of mysticism, which for him is really a theology of Christian spiritual life.

I

According to this theology, mysticism is first an experience of the divine life. St. Paul's account in II Corinthians 12:1-5 presents a model. Here Paul claims that, fourteen years prior, he "was caught up into paradise and heard secret words": whether he was in the body or out of it, he does not know. Drawing on patristic commentary, Stolz contends that Paul's being taken up into paradise means that his ecstasy returns him, to some extent, to the nearness and intimacy with God enjoyed by Adam before the fall. This leads Stolz to recover Aquinas's understanding of Adam's prelapsarian mode of knowing. For Aquinas, Adam did not have a direct and unmediated knowledge of God. He enjoyed a mediated knowledge in two ways. Like us, he grasped God's existence as the 'unmoved Mover,' the uncreated Cause of the empirical world that we know through the experience of our senses. Adam grasped God in this way by realizing that everything a human being can know is dependent on a higher reality and so finally must be traceable to an ultimate explanation. But unlike with us, God gave Adam, through a special grace, an inner illumination of the mind not natural to humanity. This grace strengthened God's image and likeness imprinted in Adam's soul, thus allowing God to be manifested with clarity.

This special grace made Adam's knowledge of God like that of the angels. Angels do not affirm God's existence by seeking an explanation for what they know in sensation. As pure spirits, they are not immersed in matter as we are, and so they have no senses. Consequently, they are able to know God more clearly and strongly than we can. They do this through their own spiritual nature which, like ours, is imprinted with the image of its Creator. The difference is that their intuition is not derived from anything exterior but from the divine image strictly interior to them. Nonetheless, there is a similarity. Just as human senses immediately grasp the objects of the external world, so angelic intellects immediately grasp God's existence. Aquinas calls this knowledge 'infused' because, bypassing sensation, it is wholly innate. Adam's knowledge of God was not identical to that of the angels because it was mediated by grace, a gift that fortified the human intellect so that it could know God in the soul's divine imprint. Still Adam did possess something of the angels' infused strength. But it was, alas, sacrificed in the fall.

This description of Adam's prelapsarian divine knowledge suggests that Paul's experience gives him a similarly angelic knowledge of God. But is this knowledge mediated like Adam's or immediate, as many Christian mystics claim? Drawing on Aquinas's doctrine of grace, Stolz argues that it is both at once. Stolz contends that God is immediately present in the soul through sanctifying grace. As a result, God dwells in the creature, and so the creature thus participates in the very divine life. This participation is effected through a habitual modification of the soul's natural powers which elevates them toward a supernatural end. It follows, therefore, that when the soul's graced powers reflect upon them-

selves, they are able to know the divine life, which is imma-
nently present in them. Although this reflection gives an
immediate divine knowledge, it does not confer a direct
grasp of the divine essence, such as one receives in the
beatific vision. Consequently, Paul's knowledge of God may
be termed mediated, since its cause is a special gift, albeit a
special gift which is the very divine life. Through this mediated immediacy, Paul's natural faculties, in reflecting on
themselves, would have enjoyed something akin to the
infused clarity of the angels. If Paul's experience is a model
of Christian mysticism, then the knowledge any Christian
mystic receives of God is essentially an experiential fulfillment of sanctifying grace.

But how does one achieve this fulfillment? Stolz's basic
definition of mysticism answers this question. As an experience of the divine life, mysticism is a process accomplished
in the sacraments. In speaking of baptism, the initiating
sacrament of Christian life, the Greek fathers emphasize
how the sacrament ontologically reforms the human person
flawed by sin. Because baptism restores the prelapsarian
likeness to the image of God in the soul, it makes possible
the process of *theosis* or divinization by which the Christian
grows into a lustrous mirror of the God-man. Building on
this view, Aquinas affirms that the sacrament's graced waters
infuse into the soul the theological and cardinal virtues.
Since these virtues orient the person to the beatific vision as
its final end, they are the causes of all authentic prayer. As
such, they enable some persons to reach a properly mystical
maturation in which cognitive knowledge of God becomes
experiential. Although extraordinary phenomena like voices,

visions, ecstasies, and stigmata can occur during this maturation, they are not prerequisites to the growth of the virtues. A Christian can develop mysticism without experiencing them. If these phenomena do occur, they are mysticism's side effects, not its causes; its causes are the sacraments of initiation, which the other sacraments, especially the Eucharist, amplify.

In Christian mysticism, therefore, if the human person's psychological consciousness develops to an unusual degree, it is first and foremost because the virtues have developed to a high degree. And as Stolz reminds us, the virtues grow because they are amplified by the Holy Spirit's seven-fold gifts. According to Aquinas, because the virtues are habits of the natural faculties, they depend upon the faculties' operation. As a work of nature, this operation impedes the virtues from actualizing their full potential in grace. For this potential to be obtained, further divine help is needed. Given in the gifts, this help is proportioned specifically to each of the virtues in order to inspire the faculties with impulses, as it were, from the Spirit. As contemplation deepens, the gifts are developed, divine inspiration is strengthened, the virtues become perfected, and the faculties experience more fully their supernatural elevation.

Of chief importance for the mystical life is the gift of wisdom. Enabling us connaturally to view things from God's perspective, it is proportioned to the theological virtue of love. Because this virtue gives us an intimate share in the divine nature that is love, wisdom grows as love grows. Neither wisdom, nor any of the other gifts, entails extraordinary psychological experience. They enable us to do the

same works as the virtues which, begun sacramentally, flour-
ish in the life of prayer. This inspiration is the same as the
analogously angelic knowledge enjoyed by both Adam and
Paul; it is the summit of the mystical life, the restored lustre
of the soul's divine image.

II

Stolz's book raises several issues important in contemporary discussion. Of particular interest is his treatment of
non-Christian mysticism. The rise of ecumenism spurred
on by the Second Vatican Council, the emerging development of theologies of world religions, and the growth of
cult movements have recently brought to the fore a dizzy-
ing plurality of spiritualities. For its part, Christian theology is being compelled to take stock, not only of them, but
also of its own distinctive claims. Although all of these
trends succeed Stolz's work by a generation, he does presage
a salutary word of theological restraint that undoubtedly
needs to be voiced amid the sometimes heady enthusiasm of
inter-religious dialogue. If he cautions against a psychological reductionism that divorces mysticism from theology, he
also cautions against a theological reductionism that rela-
tivizes the act of faith and homogenizes the notion of transcendence. As he says, when Christian mysticism becomes
a partner for analysis in the comparative study of religion,
the risk of misunderstanding it is high. The elements in
Christianity that go into forming a common basis for comparison with other religions actually spring from the grace
of Christ that is deeper and hidden. Because faith gives
access to this grace, it and it alone is the adequate herm-

eneutic for understanding Christian mysticism. One danger
in the comparative approach, therefore, is mistaking a part
of the religions under study for their whole. This danger
obtains even when religion is viewed, not merely as a socio-
cultural phenomenon, but as a grasp of the transcendent.
This last term, Stolz suggests, is analogous, if not outright
equivocal. In light of the reaction among some contemporary scholars of religion against a common religious
essence, the question that Stolz raises is especially probing:
Can any religion adequately be understood apart from the
act of fiducial assent that constitutes it?

Stolz's remarks on non-Christian mysticism are also
timely because they point to an important debate between
the two leading Catholic theologians of the twentieth century, Karl Rahner and Hans Urs von Balthasar: How inclu-
sive should Catholicism be in finding the true and the good
outside of Christianity? Stolz tends toward an exclusive
position. Christianity possesses the only authentic mysticism, he asserts, because Christ is the unique mediator
between God and humanity. Christian mysticism is not,
therefore, merely an intensification of a natural desire for
God implanted in us as a result of creation. Original sin has
fixed a gap breachable only by the explicit grace of Christ.
Whether there is good in non-Christian mysticism remains
an open question for Stolz, who is concerned about the risk
of delusion, especially from the Gnostic influences that
Christianity has long countered. One thinks readily of how
these have shaped the New Age movement. Its pantheism is
at odds with the Incarnation; its syncretism and claims to
esoteric knowledge undermine the ecclesial structure of

Revelation; and its emphasis on extraordinary psychological phenomena ignores mysticism's graced essence.[4] Sharing Stolz's concern, Balthasar's groundbreaking work in theological aesthetics underscores the uniqueness of Christ as the formal representation of the hidden God. As a result, religions that overstress the spirit become suspect, because they do not account for the redemption of the flesh. Unlike Judaism, whose appreciation of the material cosmos provides the seedbed for the Incarnation, Hinduism dispenses with form, claims Balthasar, whereas Buddhism climbs toward the divine without awaiting God's own message from above.[5]

In contrast to Stolz and Balthasar's exclusivism, Rahner emphasizes God's salvific will which, though effective only in and through Christ, is universal. Indebted to Maurice Blondel and Henri de Lubac, Rahner posits that since the cosmos is created through the divine Logos, the grace of the Incarnation operates implicitly from the very dawn of time and space.[6] Although drawing a distinction between the orders of nature and grace, he affirms the existence of only one concrete order, that of grace. Nature thus becomes a "remainder concept," useful for clarifying what humanity would be like were there no Incarnation.[7] This position

[4] See *New Dictionary of Catholic Spirituality* 704.

[5] Hans Urs von Balthasar, *The Glory of the Lord: A Theological Aesthetics*, ed. Joseph Fessio et al., 7 vols. (San Francisco: Ignatius Press, 1982-89) 1.217, 314, 336-37, 496; in Louis Dupré, "Balthasar's Theology of Aesthetic Form," *Theological Studies* 49 (1988) 299-318, at 315-16.

[6] Maurice Blondel, *Action* (1893), trans. Oliva Blanchette (Notre Dame: Notre Dame University Press, 1984); Henri de Lubac, *Augustinianism and Modern Theology* (New York: Crossroad, 2000); and *The Mystery of the Supernatural* (New York: Crossroad, 1998); both originally published in 1965.

leads Rahner to overcome Stolz's dichotomy between the unique authenticity of Christian mysticism and the mere intensification of the human person's natural desire for God. If this natural desire exists as an intrinsic moment within the order of grace, then it must be vestigially and seminally Christian.[8] Consequently, the good and the true may be found in non-Christian mysticism, although Rahner is sagacious enough to know that specifically locating them requires careful discernment. Christian mysticism functions like a mirror in which humanity can see explicitly in history the fulfillment of its natural desire for God.[9] The intensification of this desire, in some remote but authentic way, is due to the Spirit, whose virtues and gifts are anonymously infused, as it were, in every human being.[10]

Beyond these issues, Stolz also inquires into whether mysticism is rare. He suggests that this is hardly the case among devout Christians, for whom mysticism may even be considered normal. Once extraordinary psychological occurrences are dissociated from mysticism's essence, one can say that mysticism is found wherever sanctity is found. Rahner builds on this position when he embraces within the

[7] Karl Rahner, "Concerning the Relation Between Nature and Grace," in *Theological Investigations*, 23 vols. (various publishers and dates), vol.1, trans. Cornelius Ernst, 297-317, at 312-13.

[8] Rahner, "Nature and Grace," in *Theological Investigations* 4, trans. Kevin Smyth, 165-88, at 178-83.

[9] Rahner, "The Order of Redemption Within the Order of Creation," in *The Christian Commitment*, trans. Cecily Hastings (New York: Sheed and Ward, 1963) 38-74, at 49-50.

[10] Rahner, "Anonymous Christian," in *Theological Investigations* 6, trans. Karl-H. and Boniface Kruger, 390-98, at 393-94. Balthasar is critical of Rahner's position in *The Moment of Christian Witness*, trans. Richard Beckley (Glen Rock: Newman, 1969) 60-68.

concept of the mysticism of everyday life such experiences as forgiving without reward, following one's conscience despite opposition, and unconditionally loving other human beings.[11] For Stolz, those who are not mystics in this life do not embody holiness. As a result, they will have to undergo in the next life the necessary purgation that is mysticism's condition. At this point in Stolz's argument, the reader may justly wonder whether his notion of mysticism, and Rahner's also, begins to lose specific meaning. After all, not every saintly ascetic is therefore a mystic. The combination of grace and human cooperation is sufficient to achieve heroic virtue even without the existential sense of God's nearness and intimacy proper to mysticism. Consequently, Stolz overstates his case in making mysticism normal among the devout.

Nonetheless, although Stolz is wary of extraordinary experiences, he is aware that mysticism does entail distinctive psychological content. Much of his originality lies in isolating, in the gifts of the Holy Spirit, the nexus between theology and psychology. Amplifying the virtues, the gifts endow human consciousness with impulses that confer a connaturally divine knowledge. These can be empirically sensed. The gift of counsel, for instance, which is proportioned to the virtue of prudence, inspires a person to a specific decision when prudence alone is unable to discern the proper course. Prudence is not always sufficient to resolve the conflict among competing ways of proceeding. In fact, it can create a psychological deadlock precisely because it

[11] Rahner, "Everyday Things," in *Belief Today*, trans. M. H. Heelan (New York: Sheed and Ward, 1967) 39.

enables a person to see clearly the advantages and disadvantages of all possible options. Similarly, fear of the Lord, proportioned to hope, arouses in us an existential caution, lest we overly rely on our own efforts and subtly withdraw from trusting in grace. Given in the usual means of grace, the gifts cause empirically distinctive states of consciousness that are not extraordinary, either psychologically or theologically. Although every Christian who cooperates with grace knows these distinctive states to some extent, the mystic, under the influence of asceticism, knows them with Adam's prelapsarian strength. Stolz's analysis shows, therefore, that every Christian is a potential mystic, because the raw material has been sacramentally infused. But this should not lead to the inference that every devout Christian is a mystic or will become one.

In sum, this noteworthy book counters some of the reductionist trends of our time, while it underscores the importance of integrating mystical psychology into the doctrine of grace. One avenue of approaching this integration, Stolz shows, begins in Thomas's treatment of the gifts. Another might begin in Bonaventure, whose doctrine of the spiritual senses treats the interplay among the person's sensate, intellectual, and volitional faculties as they strive toward knowledge of God. This has been studied by both Balthasar and Rahner.[12] A potentially fruitful project of integration might be to examine William Meissner's seminal

[12] See Balthasar's essay on Bonaventure in *The Glory of the Lord* 2.260-362, esp. 309-26; see Rahner, "The Doctrine of the 'Spiritual Senses' in the Middle Ages, in *Theological Investigations* 16, trans. David Morland, 104-34; for a comparative study of their positions, see my "Balthasar and Rahner on the Spiritual Senses," *Theological Studies* 57 (1996) 224-41.

study *Ignatius of Loyola: The Psychology of a Saint* from the theological perspective.[13] Such a project could proceed by accepting as a set of useful hypotheses the psychological analysis that Meissner offers. It could then show how these are derived from the virtues and gifts of the Spirit and how they are compatible with the spiritual senses. It could also use the visions and ecstasies of this mystic to address the pressing question that Stolz raises: What is the theological significance of mysticism's extraordinary phenomena? Such an interdisciplinary undertaking would perhaps best honor Stolz's work, which opens up new vistas for us precisely because it creatively recovers the past wisdom of others.

[13] William W. Meissner, *Ignatius of Loyola: The Psychology of a Saint* (New Haven: Yale University Press, 1992).

TRANSLATOR'S PREFACE

This work lays no claim to be an exhaustive treatise. It is an attempt to approach the problems of mysticism from the theological angle adopted by the fathers and the medieval Scholastics. In this connection the use made of St. Paul's account of his rapture is an essential feature of the work, furnishing it with a structure entirely in harmony with the theological method of the patristic age.

If the Spanish mystics, especially St. John of the Cross, seem to receive scanty treatment in the following pages, this is not because their importance is in any way underestimated. The psychological method, which they represent, is indispensable to an integral exposition of mysticism. But it should not dominate the whole field of inquiry: otherwise the positive result will be of superficial value. Neither does the theological method pursued in this work pretend to be exclusive. However much patristic and Scholastic theologians confine themselves to the dogmatic side of mysticism, room is always left for a psychological approach to mystical phenomena. Both viewpoints, the psychological and the dogmatic, are mutually complementary. If in the present work the author insists rather on the dogmatic view, this is in keeping with his aim to reproduce the ideas of the fathers and of the Scholastics, and to provide something in the nature of a corrective to the excessive importance attached to the psychological in modern mysticism.

This book is a translation of *Theologie der Mystik* by Reverend Anselm Stolz, O.S.B., published by Friedrich Pustet, Regensburg, Germany.

AIDAN WILLIAMS

CONTENTS

CHAPTER   PAGE

I. THE TASK 1

II. THE PARADISE OF GOD 17

III. IN CHRIST 37

IV. THE DOMINION OF THE DEVIL 54

V. THE MYSTIC IN THE CHURCH 72

VI. ADAM AND MYSTICISM 87

VII. THE LADDER TO PARADISE 107

VIII. THE UNUTTERABLE WORDS 133

IX. MYSTICAL EXPERIENCE 163

X. THE PLENITUDE OF THE SPIRIT . . . 181

XI. THE GRACES OF THE CROSS 198

XII. THE KINGDOM OF THE FATHER . . . 216

XIII. CONCLUSION 233

INDEX 241

I

THE TASK

PERHAPS the theologian who undertakes to deal with the problems of mysticism will be asked first of all to show his credentials as a mystic. Such a demand presupposes that there can be a theologian who is not mystic as well. At this stage it is not proposed to question the justice of such a distinction: attention is merely called to the fact that the relation between mysticism and theology is itself a problem, that consequently the theologian who finds himself confronted with questions of mysticism must at the outset explain the standpoint from which he makes his approach to the subject.

Even if theology and mysticism were absolutely distinct, the theologian would still be called upon to discuss what is usually understood by the term mysticism. For the concern of mysticism is surely with occurrences in religious life, at times also with externally perceptible phenomena of that life. These must be justified, their bearing on Christian life indicated, their foundations examined. This is a theological task. Moreover, it is the office of the theologian to point out where religious life begins to be heretical, where the frontiers of Christian mysticism are situated. And he must give to mysticism, so far as it manifests itself outwardly, some interpretation, that is, he must estimate its value in reference to what theology understands by man, by the Church, and possibly by other objects of faith also. The more closely mysticism and theology are connected, the more the theologian must concern himself with the former in the aspects mentioned.

Father Augustin Poulain, whose widely known work, *The Graces of Interior Prayer*, has acquired notable importance for the scientific treatment of mystical questions, distinguishes a twofold method, the descriptive and the speculative. The descriptive method describes individual mystical experiences and arranges them in order. Father Poulain's book has become a classic in the use he made of this method. Its justification cannot be seriously questioned, especially where, as is the case with Father Poulain, the end visualized is primarily practical. He sets out to provide "photographs" of prayer-states, from which it may be possible to recognize whether a soul, detecting something similar in itself, is on the right road or not. From a theological standpoint this method is obviously not complete. Poulain's work should not, without qualification, be called a treatise on mystical theology.

For a theologian, the source of knowledge is not merely what is experienced by the senses. The subject of theology is principally something transcending nature, something beyond the range of normal sense experience. Hence the theologian's interest in mysticism lies deeper than that of the psychologist, who simply records and analyzes. As the task of the speculative method, Poulain proposes the systematization of mystical happenings and the explanation of their relationship to natural dispositions and also to grace and the gifts of the Holy Ghost. The task of the theologian, the dogmatic theologian in particular, is thus at least partially indicated. Poulain does not take up this task: in his opinion it has already been accomplished in theological works not to be improved upon.

This may sound disheartening, especially as recently the theological side of mysticism has been dealt with exhaustively on the lines of traditional Scholastic theology. We need only recall in this connection the French Dominican theologians, Gardeil, Garrigou-Lagrange, Joret.[1] Nevertheless it is worth while facing the task again, not only to synthesize in its essential points what has been elaborated already, but also and chiefly to open a way for linking these questions

[1] A. Gardeil, O.P., *La structure de l'âme et l'expérience mystique*, 1927; R. Garrigou-Lagrange, O.P., *Christian Perfection and Contemplation*, 1937; D. Joret, O.P., *La contemplation mystique*, 1923.

of mystical theology with the newly awakening patristic theology. In mystical theology this procedure
is necessary. From the early ages of the Church down
to our day the language of mysticism has remained
substantially the same. In it are to be found theological expressions which originate to some extent from
non-Christian mysticism and which have acquired
their specifically Christian meaning in the theology
of the early Church. The theologians whom Poulain
has in mind, as likewise modern speculative studies in
mysticism, treat of mystical questions on the basis of
an almost exclusively Scholastic understanding of these
concepts. Thus it is clear that one section only of the
theological questions affecting mysticism is covered.
To develop a theology of mysticism based on a patristic understanding of the traditional concepts is so vast
an undertaking that here only a slight attempt can be
made to fuse patristic and Scholastic theology into
some such system. We need to find a suitable starting
point for this attempt.

Today whoever takes his bearings in mysticism discovers that he has been led out on to a battlefield. The
conflict seems to be about fundamental questions. A
theology of mysticism cannot begin with an exposition
of the pros and cons of this dispute. The danger of losing perspective is too great. Another consideration
arises: perhaps the present-day conflict over fundamental questions in mysticism does not after all touch

the really fundamental issues. The dispute is entirely conditioned by circumstances of time, arising as it does from a concrete situation in the last century, from reaction against the excessive value attached to purely discursive and meditative prayer and from the effort to restore to mysticism its place in Christian life.[2] For a preliminary orientation we should in any case summarize briefly the theology of mysticism in its present-day position. Then a starting point must be looked for, outside the modern conflict. Not that this latter is to be in any sense disregarded; it is a question of adopting the right attitude toward it.

A summary of the position today as far as mysticism is concerned should reveal what is generally, or at least almost generally, admitted, and further what is the subject of dispute.

A certain unanimity is discernible in the various definitions of the essence of the mystical. Writers on this subject commonly acknowledge that there belongs essentially to mystical life an experimental realization of God's presence and of His activity within the soul.[3] According to Poulain, the characteristic difference between the mystical state and the recollection of ordinary prayer lies in the fact that in mystical

[2] C. Butler, O.S.B., *Western Mysticism*, 1927, pp. xii f.
[3] Later observations will show that a more exact conceptual definition of the mystical is possible, though the one given above is correct in its general wording: it will, therefore, be accepted provisionally in what follows.

prayer God not only helps man to think of Him and to recall His presence, but gives man an experimental knowledge of that presence. "In a word, He makes us feel that we really enter into communication with Him." [4] What this experience signifies and how it is to be understood, will be explained later.

There is further unanimity on the point that revelations, visions, stigmata, and the like do not belong to the essence of mystical life. Indeed these are often of doubtful value. "Extraordinary phenomena are no proof of intimacy with God and of holiness; they are just as little a regular means of attaining to moral perfection and close union with God. The mystics have called attention rather to the danger easily resulting when phenomena of this kind, in one's own case or in that of others, are overvalued." [5]

Far-reaching agreement prevails also in defining the nature of mystical knowledge, of mystical contem-

[4] A. Poulain, S.J., *The Graces of Interior Prayer*, 1912, p. 65. Similarly E. Krebs, *Grundfragen der kirchlichen Mystik*, 1921, p. 36: "Mysticism in the sense of the Church is the experience or awareness of a union effected by grace between the soul and God. . . . Summing it up in three words, we can describe this experience as *cognitio Dei experimentalis*, as a consciousness of God's nearness." According to A. Mager, O.S.B., by mysticism is understood an "extraordinary kind of religious activity centering round an immediate experience of God" (*Mystik als Lehre und Leben*, 1934, p. 25). A good summary of present-day terminology is furnished by J. de Guibert, S.J., "Mystique," in *Revue d'ascétique et de mystique*, 1926, pp. 3–16. Cf. also Bremond, *Histoire littéraire du sentiment religieux* (1925), II, 585 ff.

[5] J. Zahn, *Einführung in die christliche Mystik*, 1922, p. 637. Mager, *op. cit.*, p. 187: "Today . . . there can be few people who do not reckon visions as merely concomitant phenomena of mysticism."

plation. This knowledge is distinguished in important respects from our ordinary knowledge. The latter advances step by step with the help of individual perceptions and ideas: in mystical knowledge, on the other hand, God by His presence in the soul does not, like an instructor, impart individual truths to it and elucidate them for it. More accurately we may say that the object is embraced in a unity, or better still, that the knowing subject is seized in the grasp of the object and so filled by it as to be no longer capable afterward of rendering an adequate account of the experience in words or in anything corresponding to ordinary human knowledge. Garrigou-Lagrange defines contemplation as "a simple intellectual view of the truth, superior to reasoning and accompanied by admiration." [6] This leads to the last generally accepted definition of the mystical: mystical knowledge is not a mere gaze, it is just as much self-surrendering love. "Anyone who analyzes the characteristics of the mystics, not according to the dead letter but the living spirit, will discover again and again that love constitutes the inmost core and essential basis of mystical experience." [7]

The present inquiry will show that these definitions of the mystical have rightly won general acceptance.

Divergence of view prevails chiefly in the theory

[6] *Christian Perfection*, p. 45.
[7] Mager, *op. cit.*, p. 62.

of mysticism regarding two questions: the theological question of the relation between mystical graces and ordinary Christian life, and the psychological question concerning the nature of the soul's activity in the mystical state.[8] Of these only the first falls within the scope of our inquiry. In the answer to the question how mysticism is related to ordinary Christian life, two schools can be distinguished. One, recognizing Poulain as its leader, posits an essential distinction between mystical and ordinary Christian life. Mysticism has in itself nothing to do with that effort toward Christian perfection which is normal and of universal obligation. It implies an extraordinary way for those specially called. Consequently this school postulates two distinct forms of prayer. According to it, there is an ordinary and an extraordinary, or mystical, prayer. That prayer or that state of soul is mystical which our own strength, even supported by grace, can never realize even in limited measure or for a short time. Hence this school maintains that contemplation is of two kinds: one we can attain through our own efforts, by practice and asceticism (acquired contemplation); the other, infused, is the fruit of a special grace (mystical contemplation). The second school, at present represented chiefly by Garrigou-Lagrange, conceives the mystical life as the normal crowning of that state of grace accorded to all

[8] Cf. the article, "Mystique, questions théologiques," in the *Dictionnaire de théologie catholique*, X, 2660 ff.

Christians. Mysticism and ordinary Christian life are thus not specifically distinct, but differ only in degree. Accordingly the theory of two essentially distinct forms of contemplation is also rejected.

From the different attitudes adopted toward the relation between mysticism and the Christian ideal of life, there follows naturally divergence in the concept of vocation to mysticism. In the mind of the former school, not every Christian is called to the mystical life: according to the other school, because of sanctifying grace, everyone carries within himself the seed of mystical life and therefore the vocation to it.

Another disputed question ranges round the nature of mystical contemplation. Does it remain entirely on the level of knowledge by faith or does it in some way rise above that level, that is, does the soul in mystical contemplation enter into direct contact with the essence of God or only with His gifts?

Finally, the relation between love and knowledge in mystical contemplation is also disputed; does the primacy belong to love or to knowledge?

This brief review of the present position of mystical theology shows that the problems of mysticism are viewed within a definite theological setting. Any connection with questions of theological anthropology or with teaching about the Church and the redemption, etc., is scarcely apparent. Although Garrigou-Lagrange (in his *Christian Perfection and Contempla-*

tion) sets out to build up a theology of mysticism on a broader dogmatic basis, he does not develop in essentials anything more than dogmatic teaching on faith, grace, charity, and the gifts of the Holy Ghost. To be sure, dogmatic foundations for the mystical life are thus provided, but the question still remains whether they are those dogmatic foundations which enlighten us about mystical life in its deepest sense.

This narrowing of the theological setting can be retraced ultimately to a more psychological attitude, especially on the part of that later Scholasticism on which modern theology consciously or unconsciously depends. In the theology of mysticism the problems affecting the psychic life of the individual are visualized almost to the exclusion of everything else. Psychological interest has, in fact, become the hall-mark of modern mysticism: "The characteristic of the mystics since the sixteenth century, notably of St. Teresa, consists in the fact that they focus their chief attention expressly on the psychic state in mystical life, not on the element of grace." [9]

For a theology of mysticism it is of paramount importance to find a starting point which will enable the theologian to emerge from this restricted area and to counter effectively the objection that he is preoccupied with the modern aspect of the problem. Obviously a beginning should be made from the

[9] Mager, *op. cit.,* p. 441.

ecclesiastical decisions on mysticism which would themselves provide an unobjectionable basis for pronouncing judgment on mystical questions. Such would be the correct method if the decisions of the extraordinary ecclesiastical *magisterium* touched on all essential and fundamental problems of mysticism. However, from the very outset this is not definitely established. Certainly the extraordinary *magisterium* deals only with questions called into doubt or disputed. A theological inquiry basing itself only on what has been defined is consequently always in danger of overlooking something essential, so long as no error has ever arisen contrary to it and no corresponding decision has been formulated.[10] At least, such a theological method, even if all the essential points of mysticism had been defined, would be conducive to a defense rather than to a theology of mysticism.

Again, our thoughts might turn to the "mystical theology" of the Areopagite, the so-called Pseudo-Dionysius, a writer of the fifth century who has been hailed as the father of Christian mysticism. Taking him as a starting point, we might perhaps arrive at an adequate understanding of mysticism. But the Areopagite is nowadays too strongly suspected of pagan neo-Platonism to permit of his being acknowledged without further ado as a trustworthy guide to Christian

---

[10] A. Stolz, O.S.B., "Neue Dogmen?" in *Bened. Monatschrift*, XVI (1934), 187–201; and W. F. Sparrow Simpson, *New Dogmas* (1936), pp. 155–61.

mysticism. It seems more advisable to go back before
Dionysius, even to the Apostolic age itself. A possibility is there provided, and indeed, according to Zahn,
in the case of him who first wrote on Christian mysticism and knew how to speak of it "from the experience
of his own heart and that of the Christian community," [11] in the case of Paul, the Apostle of the Gentiles. The well-known account given by St. Paul of
his rapture into paradise and to the third heaven has
been recognized and interpreted by Christian tradition
of all ages as descriptive of a mystical experience. It
leads directly to the heart of the mystical problem.
Even if in Paul's rapture as a concrete case we are dealing with an extraordinary phenomenon of mystical
life, yet, with the help of the commentary provided by
tradition, we can learn from it what is to be understood by mysticism according to the mind of the
Church, what its significance is, and on what bases it
rests.

In the Second Epistle to the Corinthians, St. Paul
defends and establishes his Apostolic dignity, so that
the Corinthians may have no valid reason for giving
ear to false prophets. In no respect are these latter superior to the Apostle of the Gentiles, whether in
knowledge or in unselfishness or in birth. On the contrary, Paul can boast of having labored more than
others for the Gospel and of having been deemed

[11] *Op. cit.*, p. 30

worthy to receive special marks of distinction from the Lord. His purpose is to close the mouth of adversaries who appeal to their personal association with the heavenly world. Accordingly Paul recounts the visions and revelations vouchsafed to him by God: "If I must glory (it is not expedient indeed): but I will come to visions and revelations of the Lord. I know a man in Christ above fourteen years ago (whether in the body, I know not, or out of the body, I know not; God knoweth), such a one caught up to the third heaven. And I know such a man (whether in the body, or out of the body, I know not: God knoweth): that he was caught up into paradise and heard secret words, which it is not granted to man to utter. For such an one I will glory; but for myself I will glory nothing, but in my infirmities" (II Cor. 12:1–5).

This description given by Paul himself we may rightly consider as referring to a genuine mystical experience, a mystical experience at its highest pitch. St. Gregory of Nyssa points to Paul's rapture as the ideal condition of *theoria*,[12] and St. Thomas Aquinas in a question on contemplation says: "The highest degree of contemplation in the present life is that which Paul had in rapture, whereby he was in a middle state between the present life and the life to come." [13] Therefore theologians speak of rapture as a special de-

---

[12] Homilies on the Canticle of Canticles: homily 5.
[13] *Summa*, IIa IIae, q.180, a.5. Cf. Richard of St. Victor, *De Trinitate*, prol.

gree of the mystical life.[14] Before passing to an exposition of the sense in which this account of St. Paul's
rapture is interpreted in patristic writings, it is important, for detecting the character of modern literature
and in confirmation of what has been said above, to
show at least briefly how the greater mystical works
of the Scholastics and of more recent theology speak
of rapture in general and of St. Paul's in particular.
However, since they are all closely dependent on St.
Thomas, it will be sufficient to present the teaching of
the latter.

In the second part of his *Summa*, St. Thomas speaks
of individual groups of men who in various ways and
by divers routes are being guided toward the eternal
goal. As a particular group he treats of those having
the charismata, among which he includes rapture as a
special degree of prophecy. In his view, what is essential in rapture is the violent way in which the soul is
freed from that form of knowledge connatural to it
here on earth, knowledge based on sense perception.
A similar release from sensitive knowledge occurs, according to him, in ecstasy also, but without the vio-
lence which is a feature of rapture. The revelation with
which St. Paul was favored is explained by St. Thomas
as a fleeting immediate vision of God. It is precisely this
assumption which enables him to grasp the need for a

---

[14] E. g., Vallgornera, O.P. (d. 1665), *Mystica theologia S. Thomae*
1911), II, 243: *de oratione raptus;* Joseph a Spiritu Sancto (d. 1736),
Cursus theologiae mystico-scholasticae (1925), II, 501 and passim.

complete separation from every form of sense knowledge. It explains further the ineffable nature of Paul's experience: to express in human language the experience of the beatific vision is impossible. The separation of soul from body was, however, not complete. The soul remained, even in the moment of rapture, essentially united to the body, but was temporarily raised to that mode of knowing which is impossible in this life apart from special divine intervention. Such is substantially St. Thomas' teaching regarding the rapture of St. Paul.[15] He is interested in it primarily from a psychological standpoint: he investigates the mode of knowledge enjoyed by Paul, the relationship of soul and body in the state of rapture, etc. He makes no further pronouncements, say in reference to soteriology, such as seem to be suggested by the mention of the heavenly state.

This interpretation quite fully confirms what has been said already regarding the psychological outlook of more recent mysticism. If we wish to arrive at a deeper and more comprehensive understanding of mystical experience, we must free ourselves from this narrow psychological setting. To this end an interpretation of Paul's experience lends itself in a special way. We have here before us an experience which, as St. Thomas himself observed, is an ideal condition of

[15] *Summa*, IIa IIae, q. 175. St. Thomas treats expressly of St. Paul's rapture also in his commentary on II Cor., chap. 12.

mystical life. In explaining it, ecclesiastical doctors have passed by scarcely a single essential feature of the mystical.[16] The following chapter will follow up the hints suggested by tradition in its commentary on St. Paul's account, thus to illustrate the theological foundations of this unique mystical experience and, at the same time, of mysticism in general.

[16] Most of the fathers deal with this text not in a commentary on II Corinthians, but in connection with mystical problems.

II

THE PARADISE OF GOD

IN THE life of St. Anselm of Canterbury it is recounted how, as a boy, one night in a dream he was raised up to the royal palace of heaven, where he received a friendly welcome from the King. "Then at the Lord's command there is brought to him by the chief steward a loaf of bread gleaming white with which he fortifies himself in the presence of the Lord." The boy remained firmly convinced that he had actually been in heaven and had been strengthened by the bread of the Lord.[1]

In this narrative we perceive an echo of a theme familiar to ancient monastic literature, where we often hear of wanderings, in dream or in ecstasy, into heaven or paradise and of the tasting of heavenly food. Such a visit to heaven or paradise is a guaranty that the monk possesses the spirit of God and that he has already reached a special degree of perfection and un-

[1] *Vita S. Anselmi* by Eadmer, no. 2.

ion with God.[2] We may surmise a close connection
between such narrations and the account given by
St. Paul of his rapture into paradise. In the case of Paul
it is particularly significant that he appeals to the rapture into paradise and the third heaven as a direct cre-
dential of his Apostolate. An interpretation of his
account must therefore begin with an explanation of
the terminus of the rapture, that is, of paradise.

Today we are no longer accustomed to picture to
ourselves as still in existence the Paradise where Adam
and Eve lived in the first happy days of our race's history. Consequently the thought that Paul was trans-
ported to this Paradise does not readily occur to us.
This was not so for earlier theological tradition. St.
Ambrose (d. 397) at the very beginning of his book
De paradiso takes for granted that Paul saw the Paradise of Adam which still exists.[3] Later theologians
also hold fast to the continued existence of Paradise.
Isidore of Seville (d. 636) in his *Etymologiae* reckons
it as a province of Asia along with India, Assyria, etc.[4]

Traces of this tradition are still recognizable in the
writings of St. Thomas Aquinas. In his *Summa theologica* he devotes a special question to "the place of
the first human being." Quite in line with tradition, he

[2] Reitzenstein, *Historia monachorum und Historia Lausiaca* (1916),
pp. 121 f., 171 ff.
[3] Chap. 1, no. 1. Thus St. Irenaeus in the second century, *Adv.
haeres.*, V, v, 1.
[4] Etym., XIV, 3: *Habet autem (Asia) provincias multas et regiones,
quarum breviter nomina et situs expediam, sumpto initio a paradiso.*

regards Paradise as a terrestrial place. To the objection
that no explorer has been able so far to discover Paradise, and therefore we cannot regard it as a terrestrial
place but must understand it in a spiritual sense, he
does not give what seems to be the obvious answer:
Paradise no longer exists. He appeals rather to the fact
that Paradise, lying as it does far distant from our
regions and separated from us by high mountains,
seas, and desert places, is on that account unapproachable.[5] He furnishes also a theological foundation for
the continued existence of Paradise and expressly con-
tests the notion that it is superfluous to maintain it as
still existing since, in any case, it is no longer inhabited
by man. According to him its prolonged existence is a
constant testimony of God's goodness toward mankind; moreover, it is inhabited, namely by Henoch and
Elias, who, as Scripture testifies, were carried off into
Paradise.[6] In this way Paradise acquires a special theological value as a material place, in so far as it proclaims
unceasingly that state of grace in which God created
the first man.

Significant, too, is it that, according to St. Thomas
Aquinas, Adam was created by God outside Paradise
and introduced into it only afterward, a sign that the

[5] *Summa*, Ia, q.102, a.1 ad3. The ideas, current in antiquity, of
the land of the gods and of the dead at the end of the earth or
beyond the ocean (L. Radermacher, *Das Jenseits im Mythos der
Hellenen*, 1903, p. 72) have obviously exercised an influence on
these definitions of Paradise.

[6] *Summa*, Ia, q.102, a.2 ad3; IIa IIae, q.164, a.2 ad4.

state of man in Paradise was a grace.[7] This view of
Paradise reflects an ancient Christian, indeed Jewish,
tradition which up to the sixteenth century affirmed
the continued existence of Paradise and regarded a
denial of this fact as heresy.[8] A denial that Paradise still
exists was paralleled with a denial that the account of
Paradise is to be regarded as historical, and thus a denial
that mankind is destined to regain the perfection possessed by Adam. In fact, a person might go so far as
to say that Christ presupposes and confirms belief in
the continuance of Paradise. To the request of the
penitent thief on the cross, "Lord, remember me when
Thou shalt come into Thy kingdom," He replies:
"Amen I say to thee, this day thou shalt be with Me in
paradise" (Luke 23:43 ff.). A contemporary Jew
could understand these words only of the Paradise of
our first parents as still existing.[9]

In the teaching of tradition on Paradise we repeatedly meet the assertion that it is situated in a lofty
position. "Wherever it be," says Walafrid Strabo

[7] *Summa*, Ia, q. 102, a. 4.
[8] Cf. J. B. Gonet, *Clypeus theol. thom;* tract. de homine, disp. 2,
art. 9. Ildef. de Vuippens: *Le paradis terrestre au troisième ciel* (1925),
p. 11. For the teaching of tradition on the continued existence of
paradise, cf. also L. Atzberger, *Geschichte der christlichen Eschatologie innerhalb der vornizän. Zeit*, 1896; E. Niederhuber, *Die Eschatologie des hl. Ambrosius* (1907), pp. 52 ff. In reference to facing
eastward at prayer as an expression of longing for Paradise, cf. Döl-
ger, *Sol Salutis* (1925), pp. 220 ff.
[9] The question whether the continued existence of Paradise is
really to be admitted need not be discussed since in this place only
the relations between mystical life and life in Paradise are of significance.

(d. 849), "we know that it is a terrestrial place, separated from our lands by seas and mountains, and at a
high altitude. The waters of the great flood could not
reach it." [10] Here two conceptions are associated with
each other; even as late as the twelfth century, they are
immediately juxtaposed by Honorius of Autun. To
explain the expression "ship of life," he locates Paradise on the boundaries of the world beyond the ocean;
for the expression "ladder of heaven" he appeals to the
fact that we must mount upward from the "vale of
tears" to our heavenly home.[11] The description of
Adam's expulsion from Paradise as a fall and Henoch's
rapture as an ascent is based on a similar idea. St. Anselm (d. 1109), for example, compares our sinful condition with the happiness of Adam: "Wretched that
we are, whence have we been cast out, whither are we
driven? From what place have we fallen, into what
place have we sunk down?" [12] The high altitude of
Paradise implies that it is remote from our sinful world,
completely separated from it. The place of Paradise,
therefore, after the traditional concept, is unapproachable to men unless, like Henoch and Paul, they are
recipients of a special grace. The inaccessibility of
Paradise is still further increased by the fact that it is

[10] *Glossa Lib. Genes.*, 2, 8.
[11] *Scala coeli major*, 1 and 2.
[12] *Proslogion* chap. 1. St. Ambrose: *in Ps. 118* (4, 2): "Ejectus de
paradiso, hoc est ex illo sublimi et coelesti loco, ad quem raptus est
Paulus . . . ex illo ergo eminenti sive extra loco dejectus in terram,
deploret Adam dicens: Adhaesit pavimento anima mea."

surrounded with a circle of fire [13] or, what amounts to the same thing, its entrance is guarded by angels with fiery swords. The same thing is meant when St. Thomas says that Paradise is unapproachable especially because of the heat prevailing between it and our lands.[14] According to the notion commonly held in the early Church, Paradise is inhabited. "Today," exclaims St. John Chrysostom (d. 407) on the day of the Lord's death, "today God opened to us that Paradise which had been shut for more than five thousand years; on this day and at this hour He conducted into it the good thief and thus completed a twofold task: first of all, by opening Paradise, then, by conducting the thief into it." [15] As a result Paradise is once more accessible to mankind. Adam was able to return to it and along with him the just of the Old Testament, who had to wait for the hour of redemption in the underworld.[16]

To our mind there is no sharp distinction between

---

[13] Lactantius (d. 320), *Divin. instit.*, II, 12, 19: "After God had pronounced sentence against the sinner, He banished man from Paradise, so that he should support himself by toil, and encircled Paradise with a ring of fire, that man might no longer gain entrance to it."

[14] "Salvis spiritualis sensus mysteriis, ille locus praecipue videtur inaccessibilis propter vehementiam aestus in locis intermediis ex propinquitate solis; et hoc significatur per flammeum gladium, qui versatilis dicitur propter proprietatem motus circularis hujusmodi aestum causantis" (*Summa*, IIa IIae, q.164, a.2 ad 5).

[15] *De cruce et latrone*, hom. 1, no. 2.

[16] This return on the part of Adam and of the just of the Old Testament into Paradise is depicted in detail in the apocryphal *Gospel of Nicodemus*.

paradise and the kingdom of heaven; for earlier theology on the other hand paradise and the kingdom of
heaven are to be regarded as distinct localities corresponding to particular degrees of blessedness.[17] In so
far as Christ's redemptive work restored the state of
union with God lost by Adam, the way of the sanctified leads first of all into paradise. Since, however,
the grace of Christ goes beyond that of paradise, the
latter cannot be the final resting place of the redeemed.
According to St. Ambrose: "Paradise is indeed a permanent region of heaven, but, as it were, merely the
ground-floor, above which the heavenly kingdom,
strictly so called, is erected; it is the lower region of the
invisible heaven taken as a whole, from which the
elect, according to their respective merits, mount
sooner or later to the various higher regions or king-
doms." [18]

Theophylactus (eleventh century) expressly op-
poses the idea that paradise and the kingdom of heaven
are on an equal footing, "for no ear has heard anything of the good things of the kingdom, no eye has
seen them, neither have they entered into the heart of

[17] In the second century Irenaeus records as a tradition of the
presbyters: "Some will be taken up into heaven, others will tarry
in paradise, others again will dwell in the City: and therefore has
the Lord said that with His Father there are many mansions" (Adv.
haeres., V, xxxvi, 2). Cf. Origen, In Num., hom. 1, 3.

[18] Niederhuber, op. cit., p. 57. Referring to the words of Christ to
the good thief, St. Ambrose remarks: "Reformandum est ante quod
amissum est, ut per paradisum ad regnum perveniatur, non per regnum ad paradisum" (Ep., 71, 8); de Vuippens, op. cit., p. 19.

any man . . . but the eye of Adam has seen Paradise
and his ear heard of it." [19] Margaret Ebner, on Good
Friday of the year 1342, prayed for a departed soul;
"And so God granted me that it should be that day in
paradise and should there await the resurrection until
Easter Day, and then it would journey on to the everlasting joy of heaven." [20] As far as these differences
concern the happy state of the just in paradise and
later in the kingdom of heaven, there need be no question of any diversity in the beatific vision itself, or any
essential difference in happiness in other respects: all
that matters is that there should be external distinc-
tions, notably in place of abode.[21]

Since paradise is mentioned as the terminus of St.
Paul's rapture, we are justified in interpreting the
saint's mystical state according to the mind of tradition
from two aspects: from the life in Paradise enjoyed by
our first parents, and from the condition in which the
souls of the just are to be found prior to their final
consummation.

We must briefly consider what is meant by the
third heaven to which St. Paul refers. His interpreters
are at variance whether in his account he is speaking
of a double rapture (into the third heaven and into
paradise) or of one rapture with a twofold terminus

---

[19] *In Lucam*, chap. 23.
[20] *Offenbarungen*, edited by Ph. Strauch, 1882, p. 65.
[21] Irenaeus says of the various halting-places: "In every place they
will see God, in the measure each has merited."

or, finally, of only one rapture with a single terminus. According to the most natural explanation, Paūl is referring, not to a double rapture, but to one only. Consequently the majority of the fathers in the first five centuries also locate paradise simply in the third heaven.[22] Thus it was there, in the paradise of the third heaven, that Paul heard those ineffable words. This conjures up directly a picture of a transportation from place to place; otherwise there is no sense in locating paradise in the third heaven. Thus, according to the well-known enumeration of seven heavenly spheres, paradise would be sought in the zone of Mars. This conception, however, cannot claim any support in tradition. It seems likely that Paul merely wished to make clear that he was referring to a place which, though part of the universe, was of its nature inaccessible to us. Apart from these considerations, the Greek word ἁρπάζειν (tear away, carry off) implies that the rapture involves a transportation from place to place.

From the preceding considerations, we reach the following conclusions:

1. Tradition views St. Paul's experience and, since his rapture may be regarded as typical, the mystical life in its entirety, in close connection with life in paradise and with the life of the just who, after death, are still waiting for the consummation of things. There-

[22] Thus St. Ambrose, De paradiso, chap. 1, no. 1. Cf. de Vuippens, op. cit., pp. 99–106.

fore mystical experience can be interpreted from this
viewpoint also, at the same time leaving open the question whether the Paradise of Adam still exists or not.[23]

2. Paul's rapture was not only an extraordinary in-
terference with the life of the soul, in the sense of a
sudden deliverance from its connatural mode of knowing. Above and beyond that, it seems to have been a
transportation from one place to another, a lifting up
out of this sinful world. Of these two conclusions the
former is of special import at the moment, whereas the
latter must be taken into account for the problem of
natural mysticism.

What Paul experienced was a rapture into paradise
and along with it a temporary restoration of the union
with God which had belonged to Adam; at the same
time, in addition to this, a participation in that sense of
God's nearness, which the souls of the departed, once
they have been fully purified, enjoy even now. In
these words a remarkable feeling of expectation is expressed. Paul was raised up to share in something which
Adam possessed and, at the same time, to something
more. For the souls of the dead not only rejoice in the
possession of a paradisiac happiness which they cannot
lose but which Adam was able to lose and actually did

---

[23] The objection raised in the *Zeitschrift für kath. Theologie*, 1937,
p. 122, does not affect this argument. It does not matter that the
opinion deferring the vision after death is untenable. What is of
importance here is merely the fact that mystical life is rendered
intelligible from the paradisiac state and the condition of the soul
after death.

lose; their union with God is far superior to that of Adam since they enjoy the immediate vision of God, whereas this was still withheld from Adam in his state of probation. On the other hand they do not possess Adam's full perfection, his complete dominion over the irrational creation; nor are they yet reunited with their own bodies. It is this sense of expectation which is so marked in the entire redemptive work of Christ: as second and new Adam, He gives us what the first Adam could and should have given us; as a divine Person, by His union with human nature, He bestows upon mankind as a whole a dignity which could never have belonged to it in so far as it goes back to Adam as progenitor. In spite of this, as long as we remain in the Church, journeying back to our heavenly home, we are engaged in a perpetual warfare against world, sin and death, a struggle quite foreign to Adam in Paradise.

The parallelism which holds good between the experience of the Apostle of the Gentiles and Adam's state of union with God is applicable to the mystical life in general. It has been pointed out consistently by mystical writers and survives in the modern method of treating mystical questions from a psychological view.[24] In the light of this parallelism Adam must be accepted as the mystics' ideal. This explains why those

[24] "In my opinion, however, that mode of knowledge which St. Thomas in the *Summa theologica* attributes to our first parent, Adam, resembles mystical contemplation" (Mager, *op. cit.*, p. 223).

who expound the theory of mysticism insist so much
in their explanation of the mystical upon the sense of
God's nearness possessed by Adam.[25] Especially in the
writings of Gregory the Great, who was for the Middle Ages their leading pedagogue in mysticism, this
close connection between the sinful fall from Paradise
and mysticism is clearly expressed. "From the paradisiac state the curve illustrating the relationship of
mankind to God in creation, fall, and redemption
sweeps across the fall over the mystical life to the
height of mysticism." [26] Gregory the Great repeatedly
emphasizes that Adam was created to contemplate
God, but, "expelled from the joys of Paradise, mankind has lost the power of contemplation." [27] In
contemplation man experiences to some extent a restoration to the spiritual condition of Adam.[28]

A similar thing occurs when the irrational creation is
again subjected to the mystic as it was to Adam. In the
accounts of the early fathers of monasticism, we find
often mentioned how wild beasts follow them at their
word and allow themselves to be fed like domestic
animals: "when once a man has acquired purity, everything is subjected to him as was the case with Adam in
Paradise before the fall." [29] Such figurative expressions

---

[25] E. g., Joseph a Spiritu Sancto, *op. cit.*, II, 719 ff.
[26] Lieblang, *Grundfragen der mystischen Theologie nach Gregors
d. Grossen Moralia und Ezechielhomilien,* 1934, p. 29.
[27] *Mor.,* IX, 33.
[28] Lieblang, *op. cit.,* p. 43.
[29] St. Paul the Hermit.

as those which describe man as having been hurled down from contemplation in Paradise and as mounting up by means of mystical contemplation suggest that the paradisiac state is regained in mystical union with God (as we have seen, Paradise is visualized as at a high altitude). Similarly mystical contemplation is invariably described in terms of the immediate vision of God which is the prerogative of the blessed. In the case of modern mystics no special citation is here called for.

But Gregory the Great, too, considers the beatific vision at least partially realized in the mystical life of the just.[30] According to this, then, mystical beholding lies in the direction of that knowledge which has God without any medium for its object. Thus we can indicate as characteristic of the mystical union some sort of restoration to that state of union with God which belonged to Adam; over and above this, it is to be understood as a participation in that union with God enjoyed by the souls of the departed. These conclusions must be taken into account in defining the essence of the mystical life. First of all, however, attention may be called to another parallel. Paradise, which tradition regards as still existing, is inaccessible to man confined as the latter is within nature. It is surrounded by fire. It was sin which first caused Paradise to be shut

[30] *Mor.*, XVIII, 41: "Sic quippe (sancti viri) mortificati appetunt, ut jam perfecte, si liceat, conditoris sui faciem contemplentur."

off in this particular way.[31] After the fall, God set cherubim with swords of quivering flame in front of the garden to guard the approach to the tree (Gen. 3:24). Consequently he who seeks to share in the glories of Paradise must first stride through this fire, that is, only he who has been purified in the fire can advance further into Paradise.[32] Now there stands also before the mystical union the way of purification, and the mystics do not hesitate to place this purification on the same level as that cleansing fire through which the road leads to Paradise, and to parallel the vision of God with the mystical union. If, along with earlier theology, we accept Paradise as the first halting place of the just, then this fire in front is the fire of purgatory.

The mystics, in fact, describe the way of purification simply as purgatory on earth. "Those who have fallen asleep in a state of grace do not obtain the crown until they have been cleansed in purgatory, paying their debt in its potent flames and laying down the burden of their vices. For these (venial sins) are indeed in this life compatible with the state of grace; they cannot, however, be associated with grace consummated in glory, into which nothing defiled can

[31] "Cujus loci post peccatum hominis aditus interclusus est; septus est enim undique romphea flammea, id est, muro igneo accinctus, ita ut ejus cum coelo pene jungat incendium." St. Isidore: *Etymol.*, XIV, 3. In Dante's description, paradise lies on the Mount of Purgatory and is encircled by a ring of fire.
[32] "Omnes oportet per ignem probari, quicumque ad paradisum redire desiderant" (St. Ambrose, *in Ps. 118*, serm. 20).

enter. In like manner in this life also, there is no contemplation possible without a previous purification, a
purgatory on earth. Just as natural death must precede
the permanent, immediate vision of God, so must mystical death precede contemplation." [33] This parallelism between mystical purification and the cleansing of
the soul in the next world is completed by the description of contemplation as a mystical grave in which the
soul hides from the world and dies to it.[34] Accordingly,
therefore, in the evolution of Christian life the way of
purification and of union in the mystical sphere corresponds to death, purgatory, and the subsequent vision
of God.

So far we have established that, according to the
witness of tradition, mystical union can be explained in
the light of the paradisiac state of union with God and
the beatific vision, while the antecedent purification
can be interpreted in terms of the cleansing effected by
Christian death and penance in the next world. Thus

[33] Joseph a Spiritu Sancto, *op. cit.*, II, 6. Cf. Garrigou-Lagrange,
op. cit., p. 356: "These painful purifications, which are a sort of anticipated purgatory, belong to the mystical order, properly so called.
Wholly generous souls are purified by the Holy Ghost while they
are on earth, to such an extent that they do not, through their own
fault, have to undergo after death the meritless purification of purgatory. Ordinarily we must pass through this crucible in one way or
another; either in this life while meriting, or in the life to come
without meriting."

[34] St. Gregory the Great, *Mor.*, V, 6: "Divine contemplation is a
grave of the spirit in which the soul hides. . . . Thus he who seeks
death rejoices when he finds the grave; so, too, he who intends to
mortify himself will be glad to discover the quietude of contemplation."

we are at once provided with the preliminary conditions for determining our attitude toward the question
of the relation between the mystical life and the ideal
of Christian life, a question which plays so significant
a part in modern discussions on mysticism.

The tenor of the question is: What relationship
holds good between the Christian ideal of perfection
and mysticism? Is mystical life the normal terminus of
every perfect Christian life, so that a lack of mysticism
implies something wanting to Christian perfection, or
are there two kinds of Christian perfection? In the introductory chapter we noted the two answers given by
those who expound the theory of mysticism. What
has been said about the relation of the mystical to
Adam's state of grace and that of souls preparing for
their consummation seems to involve the admission of
a mystical life for all men. Every Christian, so far as he
shares in the redemptive work of Christ, is undoubtedly invited to a restoration of the lost grace of
Paradise and to the vision of God. In the grace of redemption bestowed upon him by the sacrament of
baptism, a man must be granted the capacity for attaining to the highest mystical union, since mystical
union and the full evolution of justifying grace mean
one and the same thing. We must agree with Garrigou-
Lagrange. According to his opinion, all men are called
to the mystical life even as they are to the vision of
God, for in sanctifying grace each bears within him-

self the proper and essential principle of the mystical.[35] The fact that, in spite of this, all men do not reach the mystical life and that those who do are relatively few in number, comes about because so many Christians do not achieve, in accordance with their state, the perfection which they should achieve. Otherwise the "general and remote" vocation to mystical life which is granted to all in virtue of sanctifying grace would be transformed into a "personal and proximate" summons.[36]

This view is confirmed by what psychology is able to tell us about the beginnings of contemplation. Experience has shown "that with certain regularity contemplation commences when definite conditions are realized. Only it is extraordinarily difficult to discover where the barriers lie as far as the soul is concerned. . . . Once these have been detected and removed, contemplation makes its entry." [37] Although Father Mager is of the opinion that mystical prayer is something specifically distinct from ordinary prayer, he calls mysticism abnormal only because "actually its occurrence is relatively rare." The reason for this is

[35] Garrigou-Lagrange distinguishes a twofold vocation, one general and remote, the other personal and proximate. The former is given along with sanctifying grace; the latter depends upon faithful co-operation with grace. Cf. *op. cit.*, pp. 337 ff.

[36] As the three indications of the proximate vocation, spiritual teachers enumerate: (1) difficulties in meditation and discursive prayer; (2) disinclination for external distractions; (3) joy in loving attention to God.

[37] Mager, *op. cit.*, pp. 235 f.

not the less frequent bestowal of the grace on the part of God, "but because the Christian, whose nature is affected by original sin, seldom reaches the state of detachment in which the soul is freed from corporeal restrictions." [38]

The assertion may, therefore, be made that mystical life is on the same plane as that Christian ideal which is obligatory for every man. By this we do not mean, however, that no one can enter heaven unless he has become a mystic here on earth. Whoever has not reached the mystical state here, must in the life to come prepare in the place of purification for that consummation which will be his in the vision of God. Mysticism completes this preparation already here on earth, thus anticipating a development which the simple Christian must face after death.

Precisely against this point a difficulty may be raised, once again from St. Paul's account of his rapture. This rapture was, without doubt, an extraordinary experience. It gave him abode in paradise, anticipating the joy and consummation of Christian life after release from this body of sin. According to this it could perhaps be maintained that every Christian is indeed called to the perfection furnished by the mystical life, but that the abnormality of mysticism consists precisely in its bestowal in this present life of something which in itself is reserved for life beyond

[38] *Idem,* p. 236.

the grave; nevertheless to this anticipation everyone is not called, for it constitutes the mystical life and is accorded only to certain individuals in whose case divine providence has special designs. Another consideration lends further weight to this objection. If in mystical purification and union we are concerned with the normal development of the seed of supernatural life, then he who is endowed with mystical graces, and he alone, must be the perfect Christian. Once the terminus of the way of mystical purification has been reached, the Christian, according to this view, has anticipated his purgatory and attained perfection. Without any purgatory after death, he is able to share in the vision of God.

Yet, does not Christian instinct assert that Christians without mystical graces can be perfect? This serious objection reveals that the two schools of thought regarding the relation between the mystical and the Christian ideal are distinctly opposed to each other—and this in spite of the obvious inference to be drawn from the parallelism between life in Paradise and the vision of God enjoyed by the blessed. The objection, however, stands only so long as we maintain that external manifestation of the inner experience belongs to the essence of the mystical life. This is the decisive factor in the final answer to our question.

We have no further difficulty in admitting the possibility of mystical life for every perfect Christian here on earth, if we admit that these external manifestations, which are capable of being observed psychologically, do not belong to the essence of the mystical state. Accordingly, abnormal psychological happenings and extraordinary phenomena are neither signs nor standards of Christian holiness. Since some sort of experience belongs to mysticism, the explanation of the way this experience is to be understood must be reserved until we treat of its essential features.

From what has been said so far concerning mystical union, we gather as follows: of its nature it does not lie outside the path which Christian life must follow in every soul. It has, indeed, the same goal as the grace of justification. This is shown by the parallel between mystical union on the one hand and, on the other hand, the state of union with God enjoyed by Adam and the consummation of the just after death. In this sense it is to be associated with the connatural and progressive unfolding of sanctifying grace. Whether it is invariably bound up with perfect Christian life in this world depends on the meaning to be attached to mystical experience.

III

IN CHRIST

IN NON-CHRISTIAN mysticism the omnipresence of God plays an important part. It is the foundation on which the mystical union must be built. The Christian's relation to God is determined in last issue by the redemption effected by Jesus Christ and is on this account of a different mold from that of the non-Christian. This is the reason why in Christian mysticism the divine omnipresence alone can no longer serve as the basis for union with God. Christ's work is something more than a mere restoration of a purely natural relation between creature and Creator. The supernatural gifts, sanctifying grace, faith and charity, are the foundations of a far more intimate relationship to the heavenly Father. They implant in the soul which they render holy the seed of a union with God which is not of this world and which surpasses all understanding. Thus they furnish foundations for mystical intimacy with God which, transcending as they do this omnipresence, call for special examination, that their significance for mysticism may be made manifest. The fact that they, one and all, originate from Christ gives them a common stamp. This we can express in theological terminology by saying that our grace is not just a development of natural talent. Neither is our grace, without further qualification, one with that possessed by Adam in Paradise.[1] It is the grace of Christ. A theological explanation of God's mystical presence must take this factor into account. It would not be sufficient to explain the mystical union exclusively in terms of the relationship of creature to Creator, or of the restoration of the paradisiac state. It must be shown that the new paradisiac life springs from union with Christ. St. Paul in his account indicates that his mystical experience is determined by Christ, when he says: "I know a man in Christ."

Something which happens "in Christ" means for Paul an event belonging to that order of life which originates in Christ. From Adam on we have gone astray from our true destiny and have fallen away to sin and death. From all this the believer is rescued "in Christ." Liberated from conditions that are entirely earthbound and have been brought about by Adam, he is placed in another setting. In Christ, the second

[1] And yet it may justly be compared to that of Adam: "You (neophytes) were in fact like the first man, who was naked in Paradise and was not ashamed" (St. Cyril of Jerusalem, *Catech.*, II, 2).

Adam, a new mankind has begun: "As in Adam all die, so also in Christ all shall be made alive" (I Cor. 15:22). This state of oneness with Christ is for Paul not something quiescent and static; it is essentially a process of being drawn into the death and resurrection of Jesus. Christ as second Adam restores the human nature disfigured by the first Adam. The task of the Christian is really and truly to follow Christ. He must die the death of Christ and live His resurrection. "Knowing this, that our old man is crucified with Him, that the body of sin may be destroyed, to the end that we may serve sin no longer. For he that is dead is justified from sin. Now, if we be dead with Christ, we believe that we shall live also together with Christ. Knowing that Christ, rising again from the dead, dieth now no more. Death shall no more have dominion over Him. For in that He died to sin, He died once: but in that He liveth, He liveth unto God. So do you also reckon that you are dead to sin, but alive unto God, in Christ Jesus our Lord" (Rom. 6:6–11). Fellowship with Christ is in actuality communion with Him in His death and life. As a member of the body of Christ, the believer experiences all that befalls his Redeemer. He is crucified with Him and dies with Him; with Him he is buried and awakened from death.[2] Such is the following of Christ in its Pauline and deepest theological meaning.

[2] J. Schneider, *Die Passionsmystik des Paulus* (1929), p. 32.

This dying and rising again with Christ goes far beyond mere psychological experience; it is real suffering and actual participation in Christ's death.

This dying with Christ is accomplished in the sacrament of baptism. With incomparable profundity Paul has described the secret of what takes place at baptism: "All we who are baptized in Christ Jesus are baptized in His death" (Rom. 6:3). The waters enclose the candidate for baptism on all sides. He is brought out from one element into the other. To this outer process there corresponds an inner one; the neophyte is removed from the sphere of the flesh dominated by sin, and is incorporated as a member into the body of Christ, the new humanity. Thereby a process of dying is completed in conjunction with the death of Christ. We are baptized into His death. "Through baptism we are buried in death with Him." "In this association with Christ in His burial the power of His death is operative and brings about in the baptismal candidate death to the life he has led so far." [3] There dies in him that which has already died in Christ. Thus the death of Christ passes over to him, and, like Christ, he is dead to the flesh, the world, and sin: "we have been planted together with Christ in the likeness of His death" (Rom. 6:5).

Side by side with these words of Paul, which seem to imply that we are completely drawn into the death

[3] *Ibid.*, p. 43.

of Christ, others occur admonishing us to die, and thus defining more accurately the nature of our union with Christ. To the words, "our old man is crucified with Him that the body of sin may be destroyed" (Rom. 6:6), correspond the words, "strip yourselves of the old man with his deeds" (Col. 3:9); just as to the words, "as many of you as have been baptized in Christ have put on Christ" (Gal. 3:27), there corresponds the summons "put ye on the Lord Jesus Christ" (Rom. 13:14). These contrasting expressions bear witness that the Christian life, the root of which is implanted by the sacramental union with Christ effected by baptism, is still in a state of incompleteness. In his inmost being the Christian is raised out of the sphere of the flesh; yet, at the same time, the law of the flesh is still written in his members, and he must still pay death its due. The assimilation to Christ is thus only verging toward completion. The entire redemptive work of Christ, which was certainly not concluded by the fact of the incarnation, is mirrored again in the life of the individual Christian. The sacramental participation in His death and resurrection does not remold the whole man all at once. To begin with, only the "inward man" (Rom. 7:22) is affected by it. It remains the task of the individual, with the help of God's grace, gradually to extinguish the law of sin in his members, and to prepare for the resurrection of the flesh by means of the new life-principle bestowed on him. This it is which affords

a basis and a meaning to Christian asceticism, of which
we shall have to speak in particular at a later stage. This
asceticism is the continuous and progressive carrying
into effect of Christ's death in the case of the individual
man.

To suffer for Christ is a necessary element in the
process by which the individual is drawn into the sufferings and death of the Redeemer, and thus it belongs
essentially to Christian life. Suffering for Christ's sake
is not merely persecution at the hands of the world
hostile to Christ, for, when times are favorable to the
Church, this may be absent. It is something which is
always and of necessity bound up with Christian life:
"always bearing about in our body the mortification
of Jesus, that the life also of Jesus may be made manifest in our bodies." The Christian constantly experiences in his body the death of Christ as an
accomplished fact and as a process, but this dying, like
the passion of Christ, is valuable only as a preparation,
in so far as it heralds a renewal of life. "We who live
are always delivered unto death for Jesus' sake: that
the life of Jesus may be made manifest in our mortal
flesh" (II Cor. 4: 10 f.).

As the last words imply, for the believer fellowship
with Christ in His resurrection is an accomplished fact
already in this life. "Because of his union with Christ
and his incorporation in Him, even now life and glory
stream into him. In the midst of his passion he experi-

ences glorification. . . . Within him there is growing and advancing to maturity a new spiritual body in this present life: even if the outward physical man is chafed by all manner of suffering and woe, the inward man is renewed from day to day. In progressive stages this process of transfiguration is being perfected within him." [4] This fellowship in Christ's sufferings and glorification involves a triple death and resurrection: in baptism the neophyte dies to world, sin, and flesh, and rises in Christ for God. The entire Christian life is, however, an uninterrupted dying on the part of the old man and growing on that of the new. Not until death will the body of sin be laid down and corporeal glory be revealed in its fulness. Such is the meaning of the association of the believer with Christ in His suffering and resurrection, an association by which he is admitted to share, as a member of the body of Christ, in the life of that new humanity which begins in Him.

This fellowship with Christ is the ultimate basis of Christian mysticism. Apart from it, in the concrete situation in which we are placed, needing redemption as we do, there can be no question at all of God's nearness. This ultimate basis must always be kept in view if we are to recognize genuine mysticism in any form. Genuine mysticism is Christocentric mysticism because, owing to original sin, the distance of God from man can be bridged only by incorporation in the death

[4] Schneider, *op. cit.*, p. 65.

and resurrection of Christ. Thus Christian mysticism, that is, genuine mysticism, obtains its characteristic stamp. But this fact does not imply that there is no longer any theocentric mysticism. Rather this latter is restored by sacramental union with Christ. Christ is merely the Mediator, the way to the Father. In mysticism, Christocentric is not opposed to theocentric. Union with God can be achieved only through Christ.

This fellowship with Christ, as the basis of mystical oneness with God, is what lends a theological significance to the mystical phenomenon of stigmatization. Since St. Francis of Assisi, stigmatization has become well known. Since his time there have been, according to sound reckoning, 321 stigmatics in whom apparently divine influence has been at work. Among these are 41 men. Sixty-two have been recognized by the Church as saints or beati.[5] The stigmatic bears in his body visible tokens of Christ's crucifixion or of some other feature of the Redeemer's passion. These marks are manifest signs that the mystical union with God is built up on fellowship with Christ in His sufferings. To regard this mystical occurrence as a physical reaction to the attention focused on the bitter suffering, does not suffice to explain it theologically. Naturally such concentration must be a contributing factor. But, apart from the suffering involved, the phenomenon has a meaning and value to be found in the fact that Chris-

[5] Poulain, *op. cit.*, p. 175.

tian mysticism is thereby shielded from gliding imperceptibly into a neo-Platonic concept of union with God, attaching too little importance to union with Christ. It is no mere coincidence that stigmatization has come to the fore historically only since the time of St. Francis of Assisi, in an age when mysticism has been in constant danger of disregarding fellowship with Christ in His sufferings. Stigmatization, therefore, must be regarded as a warning sign. Considered in themselves and in their significance for their bearer, the stigmata rank below the *stigmata Jesu* (Gal. 6:17) of St. Paul, that is, below the marks of suffering which every ascetic, every perfect Christian, wears for Christ's sake. Still further do they rank below martyrdom. For these *stigmata Jesu* and martyrdom are not merely an external admonition; they are an immediate sharing on the part of their bearer in the suffering of Christ.[6]

Fellowship with Christ in His suffering and resurrection is achieved through the medium of the sacrament of baptism. May this union itself be called mystical? If so, every neophyte is a mystic in virtue of baptismal grace and the incorporation in Christ thereby implied. This is contradictory to the common opinion

---

[6] Naturally this includes always the possibility of transforming the suffering involved by stigmatization into a sharing in the passion of Christ. "The sufferings form the *essential part* of the visible stigmata. . . . There could be no reason for our bearing the symbol without having something of the reality" (Poulain, *op. cit.*, p. 174).

of ecclesiastical tradition, which demands in the case
of the mystic a measure of union with God beyond the
ordinary, one bringing with it an experience of the
divine. Here, therefore, a distinction is necessary. In a
wider sense the union with Christ resulting from baptism may be reckoned as mystical. All mysticism strives
after union with God. For the faithful this state of
union becomes in baptism a reality to a certain extent.
In this way the foundations are laid for that closer
union with God which, in the mind of tradition, is
strictly mystical. The only real mystics are persons
who, not merely quiescent in the state of union with
God accomplished by the sacrament of baptism, develop the new powers until they arrive at the stage of
"experiencing" the reality of God.[7] Alexandrian theology makes a distinction in this sense between the
πιστικός (the simple believer) and the perfect Christian,
who is also called πνευματικός, gnostic and mystic. The
simple believer keeps the commandments and fulfils
his obligations, but does not attach importance to a
more complete attainment of Christian perfection in
this life. It is this latter goal which the gnostic and
mystic strives after and obtains. In what precisely such
perfection is to be sought, especially in so far as it is

[7] "Normally only that Christian will be called a mystic in whose
case this vital union with Christ is actually accomplished, this entire
surrender of thought, sentiment and will to the heavenly Master,
this allowing oneself to be supported and determined by Him, has
reached a particularly high degree of strength and intimacy" (A.
Wickenhauser, *Die Christusmystik des hl. Paulus*, 1928, p. 61).

an experience of the divine world, will be determined later, when we come to discuss the essence of mystical experience.

If sacramental union with Christ may be described as mystical in a wider sense and as the proper basis of later mystical life, then we must admit a general vocation to the mystical life, if not also to mystical phenomena of a definitely extraordinary type. This view coincides with that of Garrigou-Lagrange, who, as is well known, regards the mystical life as the normal crowning of every Christian life. He argues from the fact that the mystical life is built up on the fundamental principle of Christian life which every Christian bears within himself, on "the grace of virtues and gifts." In Scholastic terminology this expression means exactly what we have designated as sacramental union with Christ. The difference between mystical and non-mystical life consists, according to Garrigou-Lagrange, in that the same root in the simple believer develops more in the direction of the virtues, the activity of which is after human fashion, whereas in the case of the mystic Christian life proceeds more in the direction of the gifts of the Holy Ghost with their superhuman mode of activity. We shall explain later the relation of the supernatural virtues to the gifts of the Holy Ghost. Here we merely point out that, according to Garrigou-Lagrange, the mystical life is concerned with the normal development of the supernatural principles of Christian life in a definite direction.

To deduce from these premises a general vocation to mystical life is not without a certain weakness, inasmuch as its theological presuppositions in regard to the relationship between supernatural virtues and the gifts of the Holy Ghost do not meet with general acceptance. Above all, not every theologian will grant that the gifts of wisdom and understanding are fully operative only in mystical contemplation and not in other activities of Christian life.[8] If, however, this is not certain, neither is it evident why the mystical union is the final stage of development in the state of union with God brought about by sanctifying grace. However correct may be the conclusion defended by Garrigou-Lagrange, it would be better based on the union with Christ which is common to all the faithful. Accordingly this doctrine of the believer's union with Christ does not merely proclaim that genuine mysticism presupposes a real process by which a person is drawn into the sufferings and resurrection of Christ; it implies further that the foundations are laid in every Christian for a mysticism which each can develop from his personal union with Christ.

Furthermore, we rightly conclude that Christian mysticism is essentially sacramental. This point, too, is

[8] J. de Guibert in *Revue d'ascétique et de mystique*, 1924, pp. 25 ff.

of importance in defining the essence of mystical life, although unfortunately it is often overlooked. The sacrament provides the real living nucleus out of which mystical life unfolds itself and develops up to its highest stages. No theory of Christian mysticism can abstract from this. Mysticism gains its sacramental character primarily from baptism, so far as the latter confers the first participation in the death and resurrection of the Redeemer. This amounts to asserting that the growth of mystical life is essentially determined by the operation of the sacrament of the altar, which in its essence completes the union with God effected by baptism.[9]

Nicholas Cabasilas (d. 1371), in his *Life in Christ*, is at pains to explain the primary position the Eucharist holds in regard to mystical union. Baptism has, it is true, incorporated the believer in Christ; confirmation has bestowed upon him the gifts of the Holy Ghost; but only in the Eucharist is this union with God fully actualized. Now Christ, in accordance with His promise, dwells in us and we in Him. If He finds any stain in us, He blots it out; with His luster He fills our soul's entire abode. "We are penetrated through and through by Him and form one spirit in Him. Body, soul, the soul's faculties, are one and all spiritu-

[9] St. Thomas says of the Eucharist: "Omnia alia sacramenta ordinari videntur ad hoc sacramentum, sicut ad finem" (*Summa*, IIIa, q.65, a.3).

alized, for we are bound to Him, soul to soul, body to
body, blood to blood." [10] This is not the place to develop, with greater theological profundity, the relation between baptism and the Eucharist. We merely
point out that the Eucharist as a sharing in Christ's
sacrifice anticipates in sacramental manner the union
with God one day to be realized, and establishes between a Christian and the heavenly Father that intimacy which the head of the mystical body enjoys
uninterruptedly.[11] Thus the Eucharist, as the perfect
fulfilment of what is given at baptism, is the proper
sacrament of mysticism. We have only to read the
sermons of the mystics on the most august sacrament
of the altar to be convinced that they have recognized
the importance of the Eucharist for liberating from sin
and effecting union with the Lord. "I give Myself to
thee and take thee from thyself; thou losest thyself and
art changed into Me." [12] The *Septililium* of St. Dorothy (d. 1394) assigns to the Holy Eucharist a prominent place among the seven gifts in which the saint
takes special delight, ranking it after charity and the
mission of the Holy Ghost.[13] It is therefore no coincidence that devotion to the sacrament of the altar was

---

[10] Nicolas Cabasilas, *La vie en Jesus-Christ*, 1931, p. 100.
[11] H. Keller, O.S.B., "Kirche als Kultgemeinschaft" in *Bened. Monatschrift*, 1935, p. 359.
[12] Heinrich Seuse, O.P., *Deutsche Schriften*, 1926, p. 272.
[13] "Septililium B. Dorotheae," in *Analect. Bolland.*, II (1883), 381 ff.

notably furthered precisely by the mystics, who in their yearning for the vision of God found a particular joy in contemplating the Lord in the host.[14] To understand the Eucharist as the sacrament of mysticism, a person can begin with the fact that it conveys to the soul Christ in person, and thus effects the highest degree of union with God. Thus, however, one aspect only is thrown into relief, and the essential nature of the union with God achieved by the Eucharist is not sufficiently indicated. The fellowship with Christ resulting from baptism leaves behind, as we have seen, a sense of tension in Christian life, removed as this is from the world and sin, but not yet free from all their influences. The law of sin reigns in the members of the Christian as long as he lives in this world. Complete intimacy with the Father, such as the human nature of the Redeemer enjoys, is consequently as yet impeded.

By causing a participation in Christ's death, the Eucharist gives, in a sacramental manner, access to the Father. "The 'memorial' of (Christ's) death, resurrection, and ascension in the mass involves for the believer his own rapture from this world." [15] In it the future union, "when we shall be taken up to meet Christ, into the air" (I Thess. 4:16), is anticipated, that union

[14] E. Dumoutet, *Le désir de voir l'hostie et les origines de la dévotion au saint Sacrement,* 1926, pp. 16 f.
[15] Keller, *op. cit.,* p. 355.

in which, freed from the world by the Lord, we shall be gathered into His kingdom.[16] It is this same process which Henry Seuse calls in his own idiom "losing oneself" and "being transformed into Christ." Thus in the sacrament of the Eucharist the consummation earnestly desired by the mystic receives actuality. Participation in the Eucharist is therefore not merely one means among others toward mystical union: rising as it does on the foundations of the grace bestowed in baptism, it is much more the actual achievement of that mystical "oneness," to which so far in the believer there can be only a more or less powerful reaction. Hence the mere "reception" of the Eucharist, the bare participation in the sacrifice of the mass, does not of itself make the mystic. "How few there are who plumb the depths of that which they receive! Commonly they approach quite like the rest in a mere unrecollected manner and consequently, even as they approach empty, so do they withdraw without grace; they do not savor the food in such a way as to ponder over what they therein receive." [17] Besides the mere reception there must be the "experience." This, too, according to what we have said, will be dependent in its inmost meaning on the sacramental actuality. Here

---

[16] On this account St. Ignatius gives expression to his yearning for martyrdom, i. e., deliverance from this world, in words which seem to refer to the Eucharist: "I find no delight in transitory food or in the joys of this world. I long for the bread of God, which is the flesh of Jesus Christ, the Son of David; I long for the drink of His blood, for everlasting Love" (*Ad Romanos*, 7, 3).

[17] Seuse, *op. cit.*, p. 355.

we are already reminded of the relation to the individual divine Persons into which the mystic enters, a relation that determines Christocentric mysticism to a Trinitarian form. Through Christ the mystic gains access to the Father.

So far as mystical grace completes the sacramental order, which of itself is not the subject of experience, it furnishes an experience of supernatural, sacramental life. This statement provides us even now with some accurate explanation of the nature of mystical experience. As the further development of sacramental grace, it must belong essentially to that experience of the life to come, toward which the sum-total of graces bestowed upon us in the sacraments is itself directed. What is now invisible and veiled in the sacramental order will in eternity be open to view and to experience. Mysticism anticipates this eschatological experience. It is a participation in the experience of God enjoyed by Adam in Paradise and, at the same time, in that of eternity. In this participation in the paradisiac and eschatological experience, mysticism is in harmony with the universal Christian concept of mankind: man in this world is a wanderer expelled from the Paradise of Adam; in Christ he finds the way back home once more thrown open to him; there even more glorious gifts than those he lost through Adam's sin are waiting for him. Mystical experience gives him now on earth a foretaste of the joys of the paradise of Christ, the second Adam.

IV

THE DOMINION OF THE DEVIL

S T. PAUL was carried off into paradise. Two
conclusions have been drawn from this, namely:

1. St. Paul's rapture and the mystical life in general
can be explained in terms of life in paradise and of the
life of the just after death.

2. Besides the psychological experience involved,
this rapture of St. Paul implies a transportation from
place to place, a being raised up out of the world of
sin.

This last point is important since sacramental union
with Christ, the ultimate basis of the mystical life,
itself indicates some sort of liberation from the environment of this world. If the rapture is accepted
as a local transportation, then further conclusions may
be drawn explanatory of mystical experiences and
even of the mystical life in general, especially in its
bearings on the work of redemption performed by
Christ as liberator from the dominion of sin and of
the devil. Finally we acquire new foundations on

which to base our decision in the case of so-called natural mysticism.

From the standpoint of Western theology we are accustomed to contemplate the redemption chiefly as the removal of a juridical relationship of indebtedness toward God. We begin with the idea that sin is an insult to God, which, as a crime committed against the supreme majesty of the Lord of heaven and earth, requires a corresponding expiation, or for which God, once and for all, exacts this expiation in full. This hypothesis undoubtedly postulates the incarnation of a divine Person, who as a member of the human race, representing the rest of mankind, will be able to provide this expiation and who furthermore because of His divinity is free from sin and thus capable of acting in a manner pleasing to God, attaching to each of His acts an infinite value proportionate to His divine nature.

This conception of the redemption is given expression, for example, in St. Thomas' *Summa theologica*. St. Thomas considers the following objection against Christ's incarnation: "Through sin human nature had collapsed. For its restoration it would seem that satisfaction made by a man would be sufficient: for God cannot require from man more than man can do. Moreover He is inclined rather to be merciful than to punish. As He lays the act of sin to man's charge so can He regard it as effaced in return for a human satisfaction. Therefore it was not necessary for the restoration of human nature that the Word of God should become incarnate." This objection voices something which we have indicated as characterizing the Western idea of the redemption. Sin is a transgression, a debt, for which corresponding satisfaction must be made. God can, however, accept a purely human service as satisfaction, since He surely cannot demand more than man is in a position to provide. St. Thomas' answer to the foregoing objection is significant. He says: "Satisfaction may be said to be perfectly or imperfectly sufficient. The first is obtained when the debt and its expiation are equal, i. e., counterbalance, and in this way the satisfaction of a mere man cannot be sufficient for sin, both because the whole of human nature has been corrupted by sin, whereas the goodness of any person or persons could not make up adequately for the harm done to the whole of the nature, and also because sin committed against God has a kind of infinity from the infinity of the divine majesty, because the greater the person we offend, the more grievous the offense. Hence for perfect satisfaction it was necessary that the act of the one satisfying should have an infinite efficacy, as being of God and man." [1] Here therefore the work of

---

[1] *Summa*, IIIa, q. 1, a. 2 ad 2. The translator in quoting the *Summa theologica* has availed himself of the English version by the Dominican Fathers of the English Province; it is published in 20 vols. by Burns Oates & Washbourne, London, 1920–25.

redemption is looked upon as a service of infinite merit, recompensing for an insult infinitely great, a service such as only God incarnate could render.

This view of the redemption is thoroughly correct. We are not called upon in this place to demonstrate from the traditional teaching of the Church how completely justified it is. In what follows, when, side by side with this notion, we speak of a physical concept of the redemption, it is not with the intention of denying that St. Thomas' idea of the redemption itself postulates a physical endowment of grace in the redeemed; neither do we mean to dispute or set aside in any fashion the juridical explanation of the redemption so familiar to us. What we mean is that with this view the work of Jesus Christ as put before us in the teaching of ecclesiastical tradition is not presented in its completeness, that in a definite sense something additional is called for, something which will be of particular significance for understanding St. Paul's account and comprehending mystical union in general.

Evidently, in the concept as it finds expression to some extent in the writings of St. Thomas, a reintroduction of mankind into Paradise to complete the redemption would signify something more or less in the nature of a side issue. In the teaching of St. Thomas, the redemption proper consists in the cancellation of debt. However, if we regard the consequences of the fall less from the juridical standpoint than directly in

its concrete, historical actuality, the expulsion from
Paradise as a consequence of sin and the reintroduction into Paradise as the goal of redemption cannot be
lightly dismissed. With the internal sinful condition
of mankind there is associated on the same level externally a transition into this world from the shielding
environment of the Garden of Paradise under God's
direct tutelage. Man is excluded from God's special
guardianship and so falls beneath what is traditionally
described as the dominion of the devil. As late as the
Council of Trent this consequence of original sin, the
captivitas diaboli, is given special prominence against
Protestant errors. Through sin man has fallen beneath
the sway and bondage of the devil: he listened to the
latter's misleading advice, and has on that account
been drawn into the rebellion of the wicked angels
against God.[2]

The importance of this consideration for forming
a judgment regarding the actual position in which
man finds himself should not be overlooked. His situation is not to be regarded as though merely his own
personal relationship to God had been disturbed by
sin, in the midst of a world-order reconciled, or at
least neutral, in its bearing to God. Rather man has

---

[2] St. Leo the Great: "Nam superbia hostis antiqui non immerito
sibi in omnes homines jus tyrannicum vindicabat, nec indebito domi-
natu premebat, quos a mandato Dei spontaneos in obsequium suae
voluntatis illexerat." *Serm. 22. in Nativ. c. 3.*

allied himself with those spirits which, separated as
they are already from God, rule the cosmos. Reunion
with God is therefore more than a personal restoration of oneness with Him; it is simultaneously a process whereby man is delivered from the power of
the demons and conducted out of the cosmos controlled by them. This doctrine of the dominion exercised by the demons over the world has remained a
living force in ecclesiastical tradition.[3] It is recognizable also in St. Thomas, when, following the "holy
teachers and the Platonists," he adopts the view that
individual corporeal things are under the control of
spiritual substances, and then, with a quotation from
St. John Damascene, refers to the fact that the devil
belongs to those bands of angels "who preside over
corporeal things" (*Summa*, Ia, q. 110, a. 1 ad 3).
Thereby it is naturally conceded that man in losing
paradise passed into the devil's sphere of power and
fell beneath his sway. The devil is able to exercise an
influence over man and also over the material creation
which man makes use of and which can become for
him an incitement to sin.[4] In this hypothesis the redemption takes on the wider dimensions of a cosmic
event. The whole world must be redeemed; the devil's
sway must be broken; the absolute supremacy of God

[3] Cf. Jean Rivière, *Le dogme de la rédemption au début du moyen-
âge*, 1934.
[4] R. Maritain, *Le prince de ce monde*, 1932, p. 12.

must be completely revindicated. In this cosmic event man also plays his part in so far as he is redeemed in his personal capacity.[5]

Side by side with this cosmic view of the results of sin and the redemption corresponding to them, the recovery of personal holiness is regarded from a special angle in the physical theory of the redemption. It starts from the consideration that the state of holiness is equivalent in meaning to intimacy and oneness with God, the condition of sin to distance and separation from Him. In consequence the incarnation of a divine Person acquires a particular significance in the work of redemption. In the incarnation, this lost union between man and God is what becomes once more a reality. We can now understand more clearly why early theology fixes on the incarnation as the starting point for our redemption, whereas for the juridical theory the incarnation is, strictly speaking, only a prerequisite; it is that by which a person belonging to the human race is rendered capable of performing acts of infinite value. For the God-man oneness with God is natural; it can therefore pass over from Him to the rest of mankind once they are bound to Him physically.

[5] "As experienced by the believer, the redemption is not an event between himself, God, and Christ, apart; it is a world event in which he has his share. Unless this cosmic aspect, inseparable from the idea of the redemption current in primitive Christianity, is taken into account, it is impossible to form a correct notion of St. Paul's faith" (A. Schweitzer, *Die Mystik des Apostels Paulus*, 1930, p. 56).

But with this, the meaning of the older theory of redemption is not yet exhausted. If His humanity was itself to become the source of sanctification for the rest of men, the God-man had to reform completely the human nature assumed by Him and to deliver it from all the consequences in which distance from God has involved it. Furthermore, the power exercised over man by the demons must be broken, and human nature delivered from its thraldom to the cosmos and to the devil, lord of this world. This theory of the redemption comprises as necessary stages in the task of the Redeemer: resurrection from the dead, the journey to hell and to heaven. In the sense of the physical doctrine of redemption, there can be no question of a liberation from the yoke of sin as long as a single consequence of distance from God is not yet overcome, that is, removed physically. In accordance with the account in Genesis, bodily death is to be looked upon as the natural outcome of the estrangement from God. The God-man, the prototype and fulfiller of redemption, must therefore physically overcome death also. He must arise from the dead. Only in the vanquishment of death will our redemption be completed. The Easter liturgy sings of this victory over death: *Mors et vita duello conflixere mirando. Dux vitae mortuis regnat vivus.*

> "Together death and life
> In a strange conflict strove;

The Prince of life who died
Now lives and reigns."

The victory of Christ over death is complete. Not
only does He Himself rise from the grave: as victor
over the Prince of death, He frees also the souls of the
just of the Old Testament, who, imprisoned on the
threshold of hell, were awaiting their delivery at the
hands of Christ. That the visit to hell and the liberation of the just of the Old Testament belong to the
victory over death is explained by St. Thomas in his
exposition of the Apostles' Creed: "A man triumphs
over his enemy when he not only defeats him in the
field, but invades his domain and makes his way into
his home. But Christ had defeated the devil, vanquish-
ing him on the cross. . . . In order then to triumph
over him completely, He resolved to take away from
him his throne and to bind him in his home, that is,
hell. On this account He went down into hell, stripped
him of all his possessions, bound him and carried off
his spoil." From out of the dungeon of the Prince of
death, Christ conducts the liberated souls into paradise, the halting-place of the blessed. The ancient
Apocrypha, in which popular piety is so clearly reflected, depict in full detail the expectancy which fills
the prisoners in the under-world, the anxiety of the
Prince of death and of the devils, the victorious appearance of the Redeemer and his triumphant entry

into paradise.[6] In the art of the Eastern Church this
plastic style of representation of the victory of Christ
over the Prince of death survives down to our days,
whereas with us, because of a somewhat excessive in-
sistance on the juridical aspect of the redemption, the
realization of the importance of the descent into hell
is not so vivid.[7]

In the physical theory of redemption, the ascension
of our Lord also acquires a special meaning. We have
already remarked that man is placed within a cosmos
subject to diabolical powers. We have to fight not
only against flesh and blood, "but against principalities
and powers, against the rulers of this world of darkness, against the spirits of wickedness in the high
places" (Ephes. 6:12). The world of evil spirits en-
circles us in a mighty ring. The perfection of the
redemption requires that human nature be delivered
by the God-man from this encirclement also. This
deliverance has been accomplished in the ascension of
our Lord. By the ascension the ring has been broken
through, the separating wall of partition smashed,
heaven torn open. The glorified humanity of the Redeemer is enthroned on the right hand of the Father,
outside that cosmos to which evil has access. The
liberation from the power of death and from the power

[6] *Evangelium Nicodemi* in Tischendorf, *Evangelia apocrypha*, pp.
389 ff.
[7] H. Detzel, *Christliche Ikonographie* (1894), I, 459 ff.

of the devil is fully achieved in the humanity of the Redeemer.

These theological principles are of the utmost importance for understanding the mystical and for interpreting St. Paul's account; above all, however, for estimating the position of mankind outside the work of redemption, and for the problem of the so-called natural mysticism. We are too easily tempted to regard that intimacy with God brought about by the redemption as an intensification of a purely natural state of union with God to which we could have attained without Christ. A man, possessing only the gifts belonging to his nature and placed, without original sin, in the setting of a world not at enmity with God, would naturally perceive the need of close union with God, and could even make efforts to draw near Him. How far such strivings could meet with success need not be discussed here. For the moment it is decisive that such a position in regard to God will never be verified for man. In actual fact a purely natural good world-order does not exist. Without Christ man is subjected to the dominion of the devil. Hence the notion also of a purely natural good mysticism is called into question. Historians of religion and psychologists as such, admit a mysticism of this sort so long as they do not take their stand on the ground of revelation, and consequently are not able to grasp the actual status of the non-Christian. It is correct to say that God, because of His omnipresence, is immediately present even in the soul of the sinner. But the desire to press forward to a mystical union with God on the basis of God's omnipresence, abstracting from anything else, involves the claim that our relationship to Him apart from Christ can be normal in its form. Such, however, is not the case. Without Christ man lies under the sway of the demons and cannot extricate himself therefrom. The axiom, *extra ecclesiam nulla salus*, implies also the other: "outside the Church no mysticism." To admit a purely natural mysticism is to forget the article of faith asserting the dominion of the devil over unredeemed mankind.

Certain occurrences, some before the existence of the Church and outside Judaism, and today likewise outside the Church, especially in India, manifest a resemblance, indeed an equivalence, to genuine Christian mysticism, at least in some externals and in purely psycho-physical phenomena. Here a problem arises on a par with that of the possibility of justification for pagans before Christ and for those still at the present day outside the visible Catholic Church. To unravel this extremely difficult theological question would lead us too far from our subject. For the moment the following observations must suffice. According to the present-day position of theological science, the question of such possibilities of salvation outside the

Church must be regarded as open in many points. A book such as that of Otto Karrer's *Das Religiöse in der Menschheit* is not in the nature of a final pronouncement on the subject. The older theology (theology up to the time of the Reformation) indulges, generally speaking, in more rigorous views than modern theology. The early Christian apologists especially are inclined, when confronted with non-Christian manifestations of religion, even in the case of religious life apparently at its highest, to attribute those manifestations to diabolical activity and trickery of a wily sort rather than accept them as a species of justification on the grounds of good faith.[8] If non-Christian piety and mysticism have anything good in them, this merely natural goodness is precisely part of their weakness and danger. By means of it the Prince of this world seeks to fetter man, thus to keep him with greater security beneath his bondage. Obviously this view does not signify that, thus led astray in this fashion, the individual incurs eternal damnation. Not a few Catholic theologians admit for virtuous pagans an intermediary state between heaven and hell, similar to that for children who have died without baptism, where they lack the joys of the beatific vision, but, unlike the damned in hell, have not to suffer any pain (*poena sensus*).

[8] Especially St. Justin, *Apol.* I.

The physical theory of the redemption thus provides us with a reasonable interpretation of the local rapture in St. Paul's experience. That in his case we are not dealing with an accidental and isolated occurrence is confirmed from accounts given by other mystics. Thus St. Teresa, for instance, says: "There is another form of rapture which, though essentially the same as the last, produces different feelings in the soul. I call it the 'flight of the spirit,' for the soul suddenly feels so rapid a sense of motion that the spirit appears to hurry it away with a speed which is very alarming, especially at first . . . sometimes, so we read, (the subject) does not know where the spirit is going, who is raising it, nor how it happens. . . . In fact, I do not understand what I am talking about, but the truth is that, with the swiftness of a bullet fired from a gun, an upward flight takes place in the interior of the soul (I know no other name for it but flight). Although noiseless, it is too manifest a movement to be any illusion." [9]

[9] *The Interior Castle*, VI, 5, 10 (1902 ed., pp. 187 f.). St. Teresa's primary aim is obviously to illustrate the rapidity with which, in the flight of the spirit, the soul is raised aloft in ecstasy. That at the same time it experiences the sensation of local change is suggested by the following: "I have often thought that as, though the sun does not leave his place in the heavens, yet his rays have the power to reach the earth instantaneously, so the soul and the spirit, which make one and the same thing (like the sun and his rays) may, while remaining in its own place, through the strength of the ardour coming to it from the true Sun of Justice, send up some higher part of it above itself" (*ibid.*, p. 187).

These mystical experiences can be understood as a local transportation out of the environments of the sinful world into a sphere that is undisturbed by evil, as a recovery of the lost proximity to God in a place subject to His special protection. We find echoes of this view also in the mystical terminology of St. Gregory the Great, when he designates contemplation sometimes as *extra carnis angustias sublevari,* an elevation out of the confines of sinful flesh.[10] This aspect of rapture requires us to supplement St. Thomas' theory. He explains (*Summa,* IIa IIae, q. 175) rapture merely psychologically, as a release from sense activity. To complete this, we should add that there is question at the same time of a transportation to a place unknown to us and inaccessible to the sway of evil.[11] How this comes about and whither the subject of rapture is borne away, escapes our knowledge. Even those who, like St. Paul and St. Teresa, have themselves experienced such a rapture, are unable to provide information on these points. To the outward eye this process of being raised up out of the world of sin manifests itself often by a hovering aloft on the part of the body. Thus the physical theory of the redemp-

[10] Cf. Butler, *op. cit.,* p. 119. "Extra mundum, extra carnem fieri. Mens superior existat mundo. Extra mundum fuit" (Lieblang, *op. cit.,* pp. 131 f.).

[11] According to the ancient view this parallelism between the state of grace within and the place of abode without played a part also in the consummation. "Cum fueris in regno coelorum, tunc processus est mansionum; etsi unum regnum, diversa tamen merita sunt in regno coelorum" (St. Ambrose, *In Lucam,* V, 61).

tion furnishes a significant theological explanation of this mystical phenomenon also.

What has been said throws light on the intrinsic connection between the experience of rapture and ascension to heaven, sometimes alluded to by mystical writers when they link the rapture of Henoch, Elias, and St. Paul with the ascension of our Lord.[12]

St. Athanasius' account of the visions of St. Antony the hermit is full of meaning and very informative from a theological point of view. One day Antony felt himself rapt in spirit: he saw himself carried off through the air. But dreadful forms endeavored to hinder his passage. They let him free only when forced to admit that there was no stain in him. Returning to himself, "he forgot to eat and spent the rest of the day and the entire night sighing and praying. For he was amazed to see the number of enemies against whom we must fight and what an effort it is for us to make our way through the air."[13] Here we have a direct reference to the kingdom of evil spirits in the air, a kingdom which we cannot penetrate unless we possess the grace of Christ. This is expressed with even greater clarity in another vision: "He went out, . . . looked up, and, behold, a huge form, misshapen and frightful, standing there and reaching up to the clouds: he saw two beings mounting upward as

[12] E. g., St. Gregory the Great: *Gospel homilies*, 29, 5, 6.
[13] *Vita S. Antonii*, among the works of St. Athanasius, *MG*, XXVI, 933–35.

if they had wings. The giant stretched out his arms; some he kept back; the others flew over, and, after coming through, were then borne aloft in safety. The giant gnashed his teeth at these latter, but rejoiced over those who fell down below. Antony's mind was enlightened, and he understood that it was the passing over of souls, and that the giant standing there was the enemy, full of envy against the faithful. He seizes those who have fallen away to him, and prevents them from going through, whereas he cannot lay hold on those who have not followed him, since they pass over beyond his reach." [14] The redemption, therefore, includes a liberation from the dominion of the devil; this liberation implies a penetration of that ring of power with which the demons surround us. Christ in His ascension made the first breach in that ring. Following Him, we too can emerge from Satan's sphere of dominion. St. Paul in his rapture was, already in his earthly life, freed from this cosmos subject to the power of evil, and was able to enjoy "in paradise" the intimacy with God which is the privilege of the blessed.

St. Paul's account, which becomes more lucid in the light of the physical theory of redemption, refers indirectly to the dominion of the devil: it must consequently make questionable any belief in a purely natural "good" mysticism in a mankind, which, without

[14] *Ibid.*, col. 937.

faith in Christ, is nevertheless "good." [15] The devil's most dangerous victory is perhaps that he has succeeded in shaking our faith in his power.

[15] "Le démon a mille tours dans son sac et son grand art en ce monde où l'on ne croit presque plus, c'est de faire nier qu'il existe, car il serait une preuve de l'existence du surnaturel" ("Les faits mystérieux de Beauring" in *Études carmélitaines*, 1933, p. 11).

V

THE MYSTIC IN THE CHURCH

~~~~~~

BY ITS nature the mystical life tends to the same end as Christian perfection. Grounded as it is in Christ and maintained through Him, it is not something individualistic and isolated. The mystic belongs to the Church. What is his relation to this society and to its visible authority? It is well known that this question has not proved easy for everyone who was a mystic, or who thought he was. For its solution, St. Paul's account can again serve as a starting point.

When recounting his rapture, St. Paul speaks of it in the third person: "I know a man in Christ." That he is referring to himself in these terms is clear from the whole context of the epistle. His defense against the attacks of slanderers would lose its force and meaning had he not confronted them with his own personal evidences of grace. Jewish literature shows that other authors also employ the third person in

reference to themselves.[1] In earlier, but more especially in modern, exegesis the opinion is occasionally
met with that Paul avails himself of this style of speech
out of modesty.[2] To some extent this view may be
correct, but it does not reflect the whole tone of the
Apostle's account. It is too improbable that Paul,
when forced by his enemies to break through a reserve
which he had maintained for fourteen years, should
not have ventured now at the critical moment to
speak of himself in the first person. A comparison of
his account with other well-known and vouched for
experiences proves rather that his use of this narrative
device may be traced to the experience of a certain
dualism in Christian existence, an experience of constant recurrence in mystical union with God. As explicitly as could be desired, the saintly Pope Gregory
mentions this point in his *Dialogues* when describing
the celebrated vision of St. Benedict. This account has
a twofold value: its subject matter is the experience,
attested beyond all doubt, of a great saint and mystic,
while we are indebted for the account itself and for
its theological interpretation to one of the greatest
exponents of mysticism, St. Gregory.

One night, when St. Benedict was deep in prayer

---

[1] Strack-Billerbeck, *Kommentar zum neuen Testament aus Talmud und Midrasch* (1926), III, 531.
[2] Cf. St. John Chrysostom on this text: "The employment of the third person is a style adopted out of modesty" (Wikenhauser, *op. cit.*, p. 125).

by the window of his cell in the tower at Monte Cassino, suddenly he beheld a bright light gleaming forth, and the whole world, wrapt up as it were like a ball in a ray of sunshine, lying before his gaze. Against this straightforward account, attributed by Gregory to St. Benedict himself, Peter, the colleague of the narrator, raises his objections: "A most marvelous occurrence, which must astonish anyone. But there is one thing that was said which I cannot picture to myself, namely, that the whole world, as though beneath a ray of sunshine, was brought before his eyes. Since I have never experienced anything like that, I cannot imagine how it was possible for a man to gaze upon the whole universe." Gregory thereupon makes this objection the occasion for explaining the theological basis of the experience: "Mark well, Peter, what I say. Everything is small to a soul which sees the Creator. When the soul beholds even a little of the Creator's light, everything created grows small to it. For in the light of that vision the innermost part of the spirit expands and extends Godward so that it reaches out beyond the world. The soul of him who beholds such a vision is also raised above itself and, when it is borne aloft above itself into the divine light, it is dilated in its inmost being. Thus elevated, it sees itself below itself, and comprehends how small that is which in its lowly state it could not comprehend. . . . Is it surprising, therefore, if the man of God saw the whole world gathered together before him, for he was outside the world, raised up in the light of the Spirit? That, however, the world appeared united together before his eyes does not mean that heaven and earth have been drawn together, but rather that the spirit of the beholder has been dilated in such a way that, caught up to God, he was able to see in effortless manner everything which lies beneath God." [3] Rapture is here envisaged as an elevation of the soul above itself and above the whole created world, so that the subject sees the world and itself "beneath itself," from the standpoint of God.[4] St. Teresa, too, speaks of the experience as though the soul were divided,[5] and a person, whose holy life Father Poulain was himself able to observe, relates: "There is an inferior part of me that lives on earth, that works, suffers, and is tempted; then there is another, that lives above, far off, in an unchangeable peace, and contemplates the lower part with astonishment and compassion." [6]

This experience of a duality in one's own person acquires in St. Paul's account a further special significance, standing as it does in antithesis to the mentality of his adversaries. We can suppose that his opponents in Corinth were introducing into Christian revelation

[3] *Dialogi*, II, 35.
[4] Cf. Butler, *op. cit.*, p. 124 note, where other texts are given in which St. Gregory speaks of the dilatation of the spirit.
[5] *The Interior Castle*, VII, 1. Cf. Poulain, *op. cit.*, p. 284.
[6] Poulain, *op. cit.*, p. 285.

notions derived from Greek mystery cults. We have no occasion here to treat expressly of the nature of these mystery religions. It will be sufficient to call attention to some of their leading features, so that the basic differences between them and Christian piety and mysticism may be recognized. The Greek mystery cults proposed as their final end the deification of the initiate. Reduced to its logical conclusion, this teaching leads to the renunciation of individual personality. He who is deified consequently breaks away completely from his original existence.

Deification, the goal of the initiate, is reached by means of the immediate vision of the deity.[7] God is light; to behold this light is to be inundated and transformed by it. Hence the whole desire of the initiate is to attain to the vision of the deity, which will bestow upon him the transformation of his nature. For this he must surrender the non-divine nature which has been his so far, liberating himself from it and casting off its shackles. Ecstasy, stepping out from himself, is thus for the initiate the supreme and decisive religious experience; in ecstasy he is torn out of himself aloft to the deity. Only when, in ἐνθουσιασμός, he is filled with the deity, or when the god has entered into him, does the initiate see his longing satisfied. Now he lives no longer in this world; he has been raised up to the fellowship of the heavenly beings; his earthly existence is

[7] R. Reitzenstein, *Die hellenist. Mysterienreligionen*, 1927, p. 292.

extinguished. This deification is often represented by heavenly wanderings on the part of the soul, during the course of which entry into the divine, heavenly reality is effected. The soul experiences a lot which develops upon it, strictly speaking, only after life in this world, anticipating here in time the world to come. The initiate will not experience anything essentially new in eternity, after he has left this world entirely; it is scarcely possible that there should be anything added to what he already possesses.

We know that in these Hellenistic mysteries there can be no question of a true deification. They are states of natural or demoniacal origin, which bring on also corresponding psychic reactions after their disappearance. The attainment of this vision with its pretended deification calls for the expenditure of a vast amount of energy on the part of the initiate; everything connected with corporeal life must be silenced or dulled. Naturally this is possible only for short intervals of time: soon the soul's strength relaxes, and the "beatific" ecstasy is succeeded by a sobering return to everyday life with its emptiness and desolation. Actually, however, once the initiate has reawakened to his original life with its distance from the divine, he realizes only the more painfully the poverty of earthly existence after the blissful moments of the vision. On the other hand, he still believes in the reality of the consecration accomplished within him, and in the complete transformation which, wrought in his inmost being, raises his individual personality above the normal level of mortals. He has become a being outside and above the common society of mankind, and is no longer subordinate to any human community. On the contrary, divine as he now is, he claims the right to sit in judgment over all others. This is all the outcome of that surrender of natural and merely human personality, taught by the mystery cults.

If the statements of St. Paul in the twelfth chapter of the Second Epistle to the Corinthians are viewed against the background of these mystery cults, we must admit in the first place that the expressions are surprisingly similar to accounts of heavenly ascents, which we hear of in the mystery religions. For this reason St. Paul has been regarded as a representative of Hellenistic mystery piety.[8] But when Pauline piety is considered in its entirety, this excerpt presents a different picture, especially for estimating the decisive experience of the initiate, ecstasy. In the many Pauline epistles this is the only place where St. Paul speaks expressly of his ecstatic states, and even in this instance he does so under pressure of circumstances. For fourteen years he bore about with him his experience as a secret; now he openly reveals it to the Corinthians, whose conduct obliges him to prove the Apostolic dignity bestowed upon him by Christ. Only to defend his Apos-

[8] *Ibid.*, pp. 84 f., 88 f.

tolate does he point to his wonderful rapture into paradise. Not a word does he say to imply that every Christian must share in this extraordinary grace, that only in a similar experience does anyone become a true Christian. Nowhere in his preaching do we find instructions about how to obtain ecstatic union with God. This fact shows that, in Paul's mind, ecstatic experience is not of great moment in Christian life, that Paul is far removed from the ideas of a believer in the mysteries, who gains union with the deity only under the high pressure of ecstasy.

This essential difference between Christianty and the Hellenistic theory characterizes also the Christian teaching on the duality of the person. Definitely in St. Paul's mind there is no complete deification demanding a surrender of individual personality. Nevertheless, association with Christ gives the believer a new existence surpassing nature. He remains a creature and becomes at the same time a son of God. He goes on living in this world, but is nevertheless a citizen of another world. This conflicting situation is not the outcome of any lack in physical or moral compactness; neither is it the sign of an inferior human nature; it is identical with that tension which is found in the entire work of redemption, and similarly in each one of the redeemed, who possesses the "pledge of the Spirit" but is as yet still on the pilgrims' way far from the Lord. It is a tension of which no one is so expressly aware as the

mystic, who experiences Christian being, tastes the life
of paradise, yet is still compelled to bear the burden of
the flesh.

The tension is so extensive and so taut that St.
Paul in his mystical experience is able to say: "I live,
now not I: but Christ liveth in me" (Gal. 2:20). This
tension does not imply that the personality of the
Christian is torn asunder into an absolute duality or
that it is extinguished by self-surrender, but that communion with Christ has become the determining factor in his life. A duality in the one person of Paul is
recognizable in so far as, by actual communion with
Christ, it has been raised to a higher form of life; but
it is not entirely delivered from its original mode of
existence. Moreover, precisely the unity of the man,
weak as a man, but strong through Christ, is what enables Paul to boast of his strength in weakness. Hence
also, ecstasy is not the decisive element in Pauline
piety, but the fact that the strength of God reveals itself in a man who is still in bondage to all the weak-
nesses of this present life.

This estimate of ecstasy is in complete harmony
with the fact that Paul in his religious instructions
never indicates the method to be employed for attaining such extraordinary conditions. In contrast to
the Hellenistic accounts of the soul's wanderings in
heaven, his narrative does not enter into detail con-

cerning his experience and his visions.[9] Neither does he express any desire for a repetition of his experience. If he feels the longing "to be dissolved and to be with Christ" (Phil. 1:23), in these words he is not giving expression to a desire for rapture, but merely to that waiting for the Lord and the final liberation from the flesh which is an attitude shared by all Christians. Union with God in its extraordinary form, involving the leaving behind of corporeal life, a local transportation, the hearing of wonderful words, as occurred in the case of St. Paul, is in no sense a goal toward which Christians must strive here in their earthly existence. On the other hand, there attaches to such an experience a quite definite significance, as is shown by the fact that it is employed by St. Paul as a proof of his Apostolic dignity, a status presupposing direct intercourse with our Lord. He does not completely reject the demand for such a proof, and, if only under compulsion, makes known the marvelous graces which he has received.

Certainly we are more in the habit of connecting the occurrence on the road to Damascus and the meeting which took place between Christ and St. Paul with the latter's realization of his Apostolic office. Earlier tradition, on the contrary, shows that it was precisely

[9] Cf. B. A. Dieterich, *Eine Mithrasliturgie*, 1923, pp. 179 ff. On the whole subject: *Vorträge der Bibliothek Warburg*, 1928–29: "Über die Vorstellungen von der Himmelsreise der Seele."

his being caught up into paradise and up to the third
heaven that was felt as characteristic of his Apostolic
dignity. "Why was he caught up?" asks St. John
Chrysostom; "as I think, that he might not seem to be
inferior to the other Apostles. Because they had associated with the Lord, whereas he had not, the Lord
carried him too up into paradise, to honor him." [10]
The rapture formed the basis of St. Paul's Apostolate.
We often come across the idea that it was a way of
preparing the Apostle for his activity as a preacher.[11]
In the rapture our Lord gave the new Apostle insight
into the secrets of the Gospel, and admitted him to
close intimacy, so that Paul might be able to spread
Christ's message as an Apostle, no less fully authorized
than were the rest. If the rapture has an intrinsic connection with the Apostolate, then naturally in this
form it cannot be postulated for each individual Christian, any more than the Apostolate itself. It does not
belong to the ideal of perfection which holds good for
each Christian. On the other hand, it is part of the life
of the Church, since it takes its stand essentially on the
plane of Christian life, belonging to the organization
of the Church just as much as the Apostolate itself.
This is the dogmatic basis for the assertion, repeatedly
made already, that experiences such as raptures and vi-

[10] Homilies on II Cor.; hom. 26. *MG*, LXI, 576.
[11] Photius, *Quaest. Amphiloch.*, 200.

sions do not belong to the essence of the mystical; nevertheless they may, as charismata, obtain their definite ecclesiastical character.

The doctrine of the duality of the Christian person manifests further that the mystic remains always bound to the Church; that he is never lifted out of its sphere. Whatever heights he may reach, he continues always in this world and thus remains anchored in the Church. If, then, the highest degrees of mystical grace belong to the Church and are subordinated to it, much more must mystical life on a lower plane submit to the direction and control of the Church. Every mystical experience must be subject to the norm of the community, that is, in the case of mystical knowledge, to the teaching authority of the Church. Long ago, in opposition to Montanism, the Church rejected credence in any bestowal of the Spirit apart from and above herself. As there is no genuine mysticism outside the Church, so no mysticism goes above the Church. In mystical contemplation, visions, and ecstasies, no truths can be imparted that are contrary to the teaching of the Church, or that profess to alter or supplement this teaching in something essential.

The duality of the person explains also the experience often recorded by the mystics, according to which in some way they surrender their individual being. Such testimonies are on a par with what St. Paul

underwent and with what is described by St. Gregory
the Great as having occurred to St. Benedict. They
are entirely reconcilable with the decisions of the
Church's *magisterium*, since this latter merely repudi-
ates the notion that there is question in such cases of a
real merging of man in the divine Being. At the root of
the pronouncements made by the mystics, there lies
all the time a reality in the Pauline sense, which the
mystics can record only in an imperfect manner. Such
descriptions as they attempt must always contain an
extraordinary element. Marie Antoinette de Geuser,
to mention an example from the recent past, says of
herself: "I feel myself completely filled by God; it
seems to me as though Christ had become incarnate
within me in order to sacrifice Himself once more in
honor of the Holy Trinity. . . . I felt how the great
emptiness within me filled with love, as if totality took
the place of nothingness. I felt within myself the presence of the Spirit of love, and I was transformed by
Him into the Trinity itself." [12] If such remarks should
be understood in their immediate verbal signification,
they would be utterly false and heterodox. In actual
fact, however, they are often merely the imperfect
expression of a realization entirely supported by the
testimony of mystical tradition and based on solid
theological foundations, the realization of the duality

---

[12] *Consummata. Lettres et notes de Marie Antoinette de Geuser,*
published by Father Plus, S.J., pp. 74, 76.

in the Christian person, who lives in this world, and yet is, in a sense, deified and caught up in God.[13]

Genuine mystical experience involves no lessening of activity. The mystic knows the tension of that existence which, though still spent in the world, is already possessed by God. And since he grows ever more conscious of this typically Christian mode of living, his mystical life must also bring in its train a true inner enrichment, consolation, and encouragement for the routine of everyday life. Actually the mystics combine often enough the highest activity with a union with God of the most intimate nature.

These considerations throw new light on the nature of Christian being, the supreme evolution of which is mystical life so far as the mystic possesses in experimental manner what even the simple believer holds in the gift of grace. The duality of the person implies that, however much Christian life is bound up with earthly existence, it is also raised out of the confines of the merely natural and rational. It bestows a living and personal fellowship with God, a fellowship of a higher order, transcending nature and reason. This fellowship is granted to every Christian in virtue of his deifi-

---

[13] "Docent quidam contemplativi, beatitudinem nostram in eo consistere, ut toti a nobis et ab esse nostro creato deficiamus et transeamus in nostrum esse increatum et superessentiale. . . . Haec sententia intelligi potest, ut ipsum esse creatum non desinat secundum rem, sed solum quoad sensum et affectum contemplantis, qui ita ad Deum rapitur, ut seipsum amplius non sentiat, sed solum Deum, in quem sibi videtur transformatus" (Lessius, *De summo bono*, Bk. II, chap. 1).

cation by sanctifying grace, but the mystic experiences its significance. On the other hand—and this too is clearly revealed by the duality of the person—this union with God, even when, as in the case of St. Paul's rapture, it is intensified to an extraordinary degree, is never final and supreme; it never loses contact altogether with this world. The final union with God and complete liberation from this world remain always reserved for the life to come. Thus hope is manifestly a main feature of Christian piety. Only when Christ will appear again in glory does the Christian expect his ultimate deliverance from this world and the final experience of his deification. Since he also knows that only in union with the Church can he be acknowledged by the Lord at His second coming, he is zealous for his place in the assembly and for his relationship to the Church. Thus charity, which is indeed the strictly social virtue, becomes a distinctive mark of true mystical life. Even if the mystic should speak with the tongues of angels and should move mountains, if he had not charity he would be as sounding brass and a tinkling cymbal.

VI

ADAM AND MYSTICISM

IN MYSTICISM paradise is opened to man, who now begins to share in the life of intimacy with God which was that of our first parents. God had set Adam in Paradise "to dress it and to keep it" (Gen. 2:15), that is, to be brought by lasting contact with nature to a deeper knowledge of the Creator.[1] All the graces accorded to Adam were directed toward intercourse with God. It is true, indeed, that mystical union with God is not identical with the union enjoyed by Adam. But we cannot view the sum total of mystical graces without referring them to Adam's state of grace such as it is restored in Christ, in a different and more elevated manner.

The account in Genesis stresses as the special trait of the first man the fact that he was placed in this world as the image of God: "Let us make man to our image and likeness; and let him have dominion over the fishes

[1] St. Augustine, *De Genesi ad litt.*, VIII, 8–9.

of the sea, and the fowls of the air, and the beasts, and the whole earth, and every creeping creature that moveth upon the earth. And God created man to His own image; to the image of God He created him, male and female He created them" (Gen. 1:26 ff.). This likeness to God bestows upon man a peculiar dignity. God reigns as Lord of heaven and earth over all. Man as God's image is to occupy the position of supreme master on earth; he is marked out as lord of the earthly creation. Hence he is the last to proceed from God's creative hand. "First God built the palace, then the king himself was conducted into it." [2] Furthermore, man is the son of God, for the criterion of sonship is resemblance to the father (Gen. 5:3). This likeness to God brings man into intimate relation with God. Murder is consequently a crime against the divine Majesty and must be atoned for by death. "Whosoever shall shed man's blood, his blood shall be shed: for man was made to the image of God" (Gen. 9:6). As God's image and son, the first man lived in unalloyed happiness. Nothing disturbed his peace and his possessions or the mutual relationship of the first pair—until sin destroyed everything.

New Testament revelation has made more precise for us these statements taken directly from the account in Genesis. From the redemption and restoration effected by Christ, we can see more clearly what the

[2] St. Gregory Nazianzen, *Or.* 44, no. 4.

first man should have bequeathed to us instead of original sin, and correspondingly what he himself also possessed prior to that sin. We are taught that the divine
sonship of Adam included supernatural gifts, raising
him to a participation in the divine nature beyond that
to which he was determined by his natural being, and
thus transforming the creature, as far as status is concerned (not in equality of essence), into a true son of
God. The intrinsic nature of this supernatural sonship
must be discussed in greater detail later. We are concerned here with the special gifts that characterized
Adam's state of happiness. They, too, including dominion over irrational creation, are indispensable for
a restoration of a condition parallel with that of Adam,
that is, for the recovery of the original likeness to God.
Further, in actual fact, they play an important part in
the ideal to be achieved by mysticism.

   In his original sinless state, Adam is the ideal of human perfection. He had not, indeed, attained to his
final consummation, for he too was still waiting for the
kingdom of heaven.[3] His special endowments of grace
were built on oneness with God and grounded therein.
With the fall from God, they disappeared also. His
gifts covered the fields of theoria and praxis, that is, of
his spiritual being reaching its climax in knowledge,

   [3] Of course he was also *in statu viae:* "Posuit autem eum in paradiso sicut solem in velo, expectantem regnum coelorum, quemadmo-
dum creatura expectat revelationem filiorum Dei" (St. Ambrose,
De paradiso, chap. 1, no. 5).

and of his being in so far as it was directed toward action. The perfection of Adam's cognitive life is known in ecclesiastical tradition as the gift of knowledge (*gnosis, donum scientiae*), that of his practical life as freedom from lust (*apatheia, immunitas a concupiscentia*). The crown, or better still, the recapitulation of all Adam's graces was the gift of immortality (*donum immortalitatis*). In a certain sense the sum of all that characterized Adam and which we regain in Christ is rightly designated simply by the notion of immortality. In this term is expressed the completely supernatural and godlike character of the gifts of grace. According to ancient belief, immortality is the peculiar attribute of the divine.[4] From this point of view it is understandable that the Hellenistic mysteries with their goal of divinization pretended to confer immortality on the initiate. This wider meaning of immortality is mirrored again in Christian theology. For this latter, death signifies primarily not the separation of body and soul, as for the philosopher, but rather the separation of the soul of man from God; whereas immortality signifies union with God. Corporeal death, that is, the separation of soul and body, is conceived first as a consequence of man's separation from God. It is the dreadful symbol of a union with God that has been lost; whereas the immortality of the body is a testimony and proof of interior intimacy with God.

[4] E. Rohde, *Psyche*, II, p. 2.

This view has a profound theological justification. God alone is the being, the unique and genuine reality.[5] Consequently union with God is the only guaranty of a complete personal being. Separation from God, distance from God, is equivalent to loss of claim to one's own existence. "God is life: privation of life is death. Therefore Adam merited his death by his departure from God." [6] Hence the sinner separated from God is in reality dead, though he continues to exist as far as the body is concerned. The unending existence in the state of damnation of his soul is rightly described not as everlasting life, but everlasting death. Immortality is thus in its Christian sense the exact expression for proximity to God and union with Him. The biblical narrative describing our first parents' fate also presents death merely as the consequence of sin: that is, as long as Adam remained united to God he enjoyed corporeal immortality as well. A restoration of Adam's condition must consequently include the recovery of immortality. Here, too, the accent lies on the reunion with God, which then goes on to complete itself in the relation of body and soul. This is expressed very clearly when St. Irenaeus explains that

[5] "Tu solus ergo, domine, es, quod es, et tu es, qui es. Nam quod aliud est in toto et aliud in partibus, et in quo aliquid est mutabile, non omnino est quod est. . . . Et tu es, qui proprie et simpliciter es; quia nec habes fuisse aut futurum esse, sed tantum praesens esse nec potes cogitari aliquando non esse" (St. Anselm, *Prosl.*, 22, in dependence on St. Augustine).

[6] St. Basil, *Hom. Quod Deus non est auctor malorum.*

our first parents died on the very day they ate the forbidden fruit.[7] And if God sometimes shields the body
of a saint and mystic from corruption after death, this
grace is a visible sign that the saint has regained union
with God, and that therefore his or her body can once
again claim to share in the immortality of paradise.

Apatheia (freedom from concupiscence) signifies
that state of perfection in which the Christian is no
longer subject to the disturbing influences of the passions.[8] It can, in fact, mean the last perfection of virtuous life in the case of man.[9] The passions disturb the
harmony of human existence and drive man this way
and that against his will. Apatheia delivers him from
this instability. It actually frees him from the influence
of corporeal suffering, which can no longer upset
the balance of his spiritual dispositions. According to
Clement of Alexandria, who depicts the ideal of freedom from concupiscence with singular enthusiasm,
it is inseparably linked with the gift of knowledge.
Hence we can understand that apatheia is regarded
especially by the monk as his ideal.[10]

Later theology, especially Scholastic theology, has
considered the notion of apatheia rather from one isolated standpoint. According to this theology, apatheia
implies a release from lower concupiscence. In the

---

[7] *Adv. haeres.*, V, 23.

[8] Bardy, "Apatheia" in *Dictionnaire de spiritualité*, I, 727 ff.

[9] Reitzenstein, *Historia monachorum*, p. 141.

[10] Clement of Alexandria, *Stromata*, VI, 9. *Historia Lausiaca*, prol., 8.

purely natural order, man finds his lower appetitive faculties a source of disturbance, for they revolt
against the control of reason. These lower faculties
are two: sensual desire, anticipating rational deliberation or setting obstacles in its way, and the spiritual
longing of the so-called *ratio inferior*, directing itself
toward earthly temporal things and estimating them
according to natural advantage and from merely natural viewpoints. Accordingly deliverance from disordered concupiscence signifies that the latter never
blocks the way to rational deliberation, never strives
against it, and never urges it on to evil or holds it back
from good. The fathers and theologians regard the
fact that Adam and Eve were not ashamed of their
nakedness as a special proof that they were free from
disordered concupiscence.

As can be understood, the recovery of this apatheia
plays an important role in mysticism. It marks out the
paths of purification of the senses and of the spirit,
which the mystic must traverse if he is to attain to the
contemplation of God. We must deal thoroughly with
this point later on in connection with the relationship
between asceticism and mysticism. Echoes of apatheia
are to be heard also in the exhortations of the mystics
urging withdrawal from "noisy thoughts" in order to
gain experience of God. When St. Anselm begins his
Proslogion with the words: "Arise, son of man, flee
awhile from thine occupation, hide thyself a little from

noisy thoughts," at the back of his mind lies the idea
that contemplation demands a liberation from the passions.[11]

Closely connected with this complete control by
man over his own appetites is the power exercised by
him in paradise over the irrational creation about him.
Old Testament anthropology places this mastership at
the peak of all Adam's special qualities because his likeness to God is manifested in it pre-eminently. Patristic
theology links it generally with the gift of apatheia,
from the idea that man as microcosm encloses the
whole of creation within himself. Gregory the Great,
for example, explains this in reference to our Lord's
words: "Go ye into the whole world and preach the
gospel to every creature." "Man includes something
of every creature. He has existence in common with
the stones, life with the plants, sense perception with
the beasts, knowledge with the angels. The gospel is
preached to every creature when it is proclaimed to
man alone, because then he is instructed for whose
sake everything on earth was created and to whom by
some sort of resemblance everything is related." [12]

---

[11] In his teaching on contemplation, St. Anselm depends on St.
Gregory the Great. Cf. *Revue bénédictine*, 1935, pp. 331-47. The
connection between his view and that of St. Gregory as to the prerequisites for contemplation and earlier teaching on *apatheia* is
apparent from a description of *apatheia* given by Didymus: "Qui
imperturbatam et sedantem cogitationem possidentes, laetas habent
mentes, et ab omni perturbationum tempestate tranquillas" (*De
Spiritu Sancto*, 11).

[12] Gospel homilies, 29, 2.

The connection between man and creation is thus very close. Man includes the world within himself as microcosm. On this fact the following consideration is based. If man by means of the gift of apatheia controls and directs his whole being, at the same time he controls and directs the entire universe as summarized and imaged within himself. According to the old interpretation, however, the image implies the reality of what it represents.[13] Hence it is only to be expected that the mastery which man has gained over himself should be manifested also in the macrocosm.[14] From this idea of man's dominion over creation, St. Paul's words, when he speaks of the entire creation waiting for man's redemption to be completed, acquire a new significance: in redeemed mankind creation rediscovers the governing and controlling principle immanent in it.

This traditional concept of man's relation to creation is clearly expressed by St. Thomas in the *Summa*. In a manner similar to that of St. Gregory, he points out the intrinsic connection between mankind and the rest of creation, and reduces man's dominion to the power of reasoning. According to St. Thomas, the possession of this power is what stamps man with the

[13] On this is based the well-known patristic proof: the Second Person is the image of the Father; therefore consubstantial with Him.

[14] "When once a man has acquired purity, everything is subjected to him, as was the case with Adam in Paradise before the fall." Cf. *supra*, p. 25, and St. John Chrysostom, *Hom. 22 in Genes.*, 5.

image of God. St. Thomas also says that man exercises dominion because of his resemblance to God. Thus, in St. Thomas, the relation of reason to the other powers of the soul sometimes furnishes the basis of the gift of dominion. "Over the sensitive powers as the irascible and concupiscible, reason has mastership by commanding since these obey reason in some degree. So in the state of innocence man had mastership over the animals by commanding them. But of the natural powers and the body itself man is master, not by commanding, but by using them. Thus also in the state of innocence man's mastership over plants and inanimate things consisted, not in commanding or in changing them, but in making use of them without hindrance" (*Summa*, Ia, q. 96, a. 2). Here also, from the relation of order within man (microcosm), is traced his relation to the macrocosm of the world. Thus we see the basis for the theological opinion according to which man's power over creation is closely connected with the control he exercises over himself. Furthermore, examples from the lives of the mystics go to prove that often God restores this mastery over irrational creation as a reward for self-conquest.

The last excellence possessed by Adam was the gift of knowledge.[15] Tradition discovers this extraordinary knowledge on the part of Adam in the fact that he gave the animals their names. According to the an-

[15] Origen, *Contra Celsum*, VII, 39.

cient idea, a name expresses the nature of the thing.[16]
Adam understood the nature of things and gave adequate expression to it in his speech. Adam's gift of
knowledge is revealed also in the creation of woman,
when his knowledge made manifest to him the nature
of marriage and social life. Many fathers explain the
sleep into which Adam sank when Eve was formed as
an ecstasy during which he was instructed by God in
the meaning of human society.[17] Furthermore, the
general task imposed on Adam of tending the garden
of paradise and the responsibility which he took upon
himself in regard to his posterity because of the pact
with God, presuppose in him a high degree of knowledge.

The gift of knowledge is of special significance for
mystical theology.[18] From it may be gained insight
into the essence of mystical knowledge so far as this
latter restores the state of perfection enjoyed in paradise. It is thus of prime importance to hear what tradition says on the subject of Adam's knowledge of God.

The question has been raised whether in Paradise
Adam possessed direct vision of God. This St. Thomas
denies with the remark that in such a case Adam could
no longer have sinned: the vision of God is supreme
happiness. He grants, however, that Adam's knowl-

---

[16] Dieterich, *Mithrasliturgie*, pp. 111 ff., 242.
[17] St. Augustine, *De Genesi ad litt.*, IX, 19.
[18] Cf. S. Marsili, *Giovanni Cassiano ed Evagrio Pontico*, 1936, pp. 82, 109.

edge of God was something halfway between our knowledge of Him and the future vision.[19] It was mediate like ours; Adam knew God in and from His activity. But the divine activity is manifold. We know God naturally from His visible external activity: "For the invisible things of Him from the creation of the world are clearly seen, being understood by the things that are made. His eternal power also and divinity" (Rom. 1:20). Over and above this, God is knowable in the activity which He exercises as first truth, illuminating creatures capable of knowledge, men and angels.

St. Thomas appeals to this capacity for knowing God to explain Adam's knowledge. It enabled Adam "to know God by means of internal illumination, by means of a radiation from the divine wisdom: thus he saw God, not in the visible creation, but in the spiritual image imprinted on his mind." Then St. Thomas introduces the angelic form of knowledge to explain the problem: "Man had therefore a twofold knowledge: one in which he knew God in the manner of the angels by way of internal illumination: a second in which he rediscovered God as we do in the visible creation" (*De verit.*, q. 18, a. 2). In this comparison with the angelic mode of knowledge, we should note that the reference is to their natural manner of knowing: "In the state of innocence Adam

---

[19] *Summa*, Ia, q.94, a.1.

possessed by means of grace that mode of knowledge which the angel possesses by its nature." [20] Hence the grace of knowledge raised the knowledge of the first man out of the natural order without excluding the latter: the natural knowledge of God was supplemented and ennobled by this new knowledge. This angelic form of knowledge, in Adam's case the effect of grace, is called by St. Thomas *contemplatio:* "By means of grace Adam became like an angel in his knowledge of contemplation." [21] Sinful preoccupation with external things has deprived man of his sense of the internal workings of God: "Now man was made right by God in this sense, that in him the lower powers were subjected to the higher, and the higher nature was made so as not to be impeded by the lower. Wherefore the first man was not impeded by exterior things from a clear and steady contemplation of the intelligible effects which he perceived by the radiation of the first truth, whether by a natural or by a gratuitous knowledge." [22]

St. Thomas draws further conclusions regarding the nature of Adam's knowledge of God, when dealing with the question of faith in the case of the first man. Since Adam did not as yet see the essence of God, he could have faith. According, however, to the well-known saying of St. Paul, faith presupposes hearing.

[20] *De verit.*, q. 18, a. 1 ad 12.
[21] *Ibid.*, a. 2 ad 4.
[22] *Summa*, Ia, q. 94, a. 1.

Now there is "an exterior speech by which God addresses us through preachers, and an interior locution in which he speaks to us by interior inspiration. Interior inspiration is called locution by analogy with exterior locution. Just as in exterior locution we convey to the hearer, not the thing we desire to bring to his notice, but a sign of it, that is the significative word, so by His interior inspiration God does not exhibit His essence to be contemplated, but some sign of His essence, namely a spiritual likeness of His wisdom." To illustrate this point, St. Thomas goes on to quote Psalm 84:4: "I will hear what the Lord God will speak in me." "Adam was the first of the human race to have faith, and he was instructed in the faith first of all by God; therefore he must have acquired it by interior locution." [23] Clearly the meaning here is the same as when previously St. Thomas spoke of a radiation from the first wisdom, by which Adam recognized God within himself: an interior locution in which Adam was directly aware of God addressing him. Thus this interior locution gave Adam an "experience" of God. The saint admits this in answer to the objection that faith and experience exclude each other, but goes on to describe more accurately what he means in this instance by experience. "The experience which the first man had is not like that of those who gaze on God's essence;

[23] *De verit.*, q.18, a.3. The same thought recurs in the *Summa*, IIa IIae, q.5, a.1 ad 3.

therefore it was not sufficient to dispense with the need for faith." [24] Hence the view held by St. Thomas regarding the first man's knowledge of God is quite unambiguous. Adam had no immediate vision of God; he could acquire knowledge about God from the visible creation, just as we do. In addition to that, he knew God in his own interior self, in so far as God bestowed upon him a gratuitous knowledge by way of interior locution.

This last is indeed a form of knowing which does not accrue to man from his nature. It is always a grace if God deigns to bestow Himself on man by means of interior illumination. This gratuitous knowledge can justly be paralleled with the natural knowledge of the angels, since these latter, pure spirits as they are, obtain their knowledge, not by the circuitous route of material creation, but through their own essence and from the beginning of their existence. God Himself equips them with the knowledge species corresponding to their nature, and in these they see everything which they are in any way naturally capable of seeing. Their knowledge therefore is based on an interior operation and locution on the part of God: in this, too, they are aware of God Himself, obviously in a much clearer and more convincing manner than we are on the basis of visible external things.

In developing this teaching, St. Thomas appeals

[24] *De verit.*, q. 18, a. 3 ad 3.

more than once to St. Gregory the Great. A comparison with the latter's doctrine will reveal how that of St. Thomas has its foundations in tradition. This fact is of special importance for the comparison between angelic knowledge and that of Adam and of the mystic, a comparison to which mystical writers constantly refer.

"After the first parent of the human race had been exiled from the joys of paradise through his own fault, he entered into the bitterness of this darkness and exile which we suffer. Having departed from himself by sin, he could no longer behold the joys of the heavenly fatherland which he had contemplated hitherto. In paradise man had been wont to enjoy the words of God and the company of the blessed angels in purity of heart and lofty contemplation. After his fall he withdrew from the spiritual light with which he had been filled. We are born of the flesh of this man in the darkness of this exile; we have heard that there is a heavenly fatherland, that the spirits of the just and perfect associate with the angels. But the carnal, not being able to discover these invisible things by experience, doubt whether that exists which they do not see with the eyes of the body. Such a doubt could not have arisen in our first parent, since, shut out from the joys of paradise as he had been, he remembered what he had lost, because he had seen it. These others can neither discover nor recall what has been heard, because, unlike him, they possess no experience of it, at least from the past." [25]

And, furthermore, these remarks shed light on the teaching of St. Thomas. They show the exact sense of the comparison with the angels; man in paradise belonged along with the heavenly spirits to the City of God in which they enjoyed intimate converse with God. There is no intention behind the comparison of transforming Adam's mode of knowledge psychologically into that of the angel. Stress is laid only on the "hearing God" with which Adam along with the angels was privileged.[26] From a purely psychological view, how far Adam's knowledge of God and mystical knowledge resemble that of the angels is theologically unimportant. The psychologist, however, must not be misled by the traditional comparison into thinking that it implies a psychological equivalence between Adam's knowledge of God and mystical knowledge on the one hand, and that of the angels on the other. St. Thomas has correctly understood the meaning of tradition when he finds what is common to the knowl-

[25] *Dialog.*, IV, 1.
[26] Richard of St. Victor (d. 1173) distinguishes six degrees of contemplation, of which the last two have as their object the truths of revelation. On this account, not because of any special activity of soul, in these two degrees man is likened to the angels: "Constat itaque supra hominem esse, et humanae rationis modum, vel capacitatem excedere, quae ad haec duo novissima contemplationum genera videntur pertinere. Unde oportuit ea ad similitudinis expressionem non tam humana, quam angelica effigie repraesentare" (*De gratia contemplationis; Benjamin Major*, IV, 1).

edge of Adam and that of the angels in "hearing God."
St. Gregory clearly indicates in what the alteration
consists which has been introduced by the fall. "Having departed out of himself by sin, he could no longer
behold the joys of the heavenly fatherland which he
had contemplated hitherto." The fall has shattered
man's spiritual concentration, so that God's activity
within him has become imperceptible or has ceased altogether. Here, too, St. Thomas is in complete agreement with St. Gregory when he says: "From a full
and clear contemplation of this spiritual activity man
is prevented in his present state because he is distracted
by the things of sense and is engaged in them." [27] This
preoccupation with external things is also the reason,
according to St. Thomas, why man now no longer
perceives God within himself. For both, therefore,
when they speak of hearing the words of God, it is a
question of an interior experience.

The comparison instituted by both these writers is
particularly important because both stress the intrinsic
connection between the graces of the primitive state.
The subordination of the lower powers to reason had
meaning only in so far as reason was able to subject itself to God without any hindrance. The cessation of
interior harmony in man involves, according to Gregory and Thomas, at once the loss of union with God
on the part of the mind. In a well-known passage, St.

[27] *Summa*, Ia, q.94, a.1.

Thomas calls special attention to this intrinsic connection between the graces of the primitive state. He says: "This rectitude consisted in his reason being subject to God, the lower powers to reason, and the body to the soul; and the first subjection, that of the reason to God, was the cause of both the second and the third, the lower powers to reason and the body to the soul; for while reason was subject to God, the lower powers remained subject to reason." [28] Immortality (in the narrower Scholastic sense), freedom from concupiscence, and dominion over irrational creation had their basis and goal in the union of the mind with God. With the disappearance of this unity, the justification for their existence was lost also.

When the mystical union is described as a restoration or imitation of the intimacy with God enjoyed in paradise, this intrinsic connection on the part of the graces of the state of innocence must not be overlooked. It, too, must play its role in mysticism. Mystical union with God cannot signify a revival of these gifts merely in isolated form; they must all acquire some sort of significance for the mystic. Christian mysticism is not something to be measured by reason alone; it is necessarily bound up with asceticism, with the submission and concentration of the lower powers. Mystical knowledge consists in an interior perception of God present and operative. Thus the definition of

[28] *Ibid.*, q.95, a.1.

mystical knowledge with which we began is theologically established from Adam's state of union with
God.

The comparison with the primitive state reveals
dogmatic foundations for many experiences in the
lives of the mystics, the theological significance of
which is not otherwise sufficiently apparent. When
they associate confidently with wild beasts, when irrational creation is subject to their bidding, when their
body after death remains intact from corruption, they
are experiencing in themselves a partial restoration of
that world-order which prevailed in Paradise. In them
are fulfilled our Lord's words by which He promised
His saints unlimited dominion over creation: "And
these signs shall follow them that believe; in My name
they shall cast out devils. They shall take up serpents;
and if they shall drink any deadly thing, it shall not
hurt them. They shall lay their hands upon the sick:
and they shall recover" (Mark 16:17 f.).

VII

THE LADDER TO PARADISE

S T. PAUL, in the account of his rapture, makes no direct mention that it overtook him while he was engaged in prayer. Nevertheless the reference to paradise suggests that there is question of an ecstasy occurring in prayer. Christian prayer is characterized by a yearning for the lost Paradise; the attitude of facing east, adopted for prayer, was regarded as an expression of this longing for Paradise as situated in that quarter.[1] Perhaps from the words following, in which St. Paul speaks of the sting of the flesh and of his thrice repeated request to the Lord, we may suppose an ecstasy during prayer. In Scripture other mystical experiences are usually connected with prayer. Thus, for example, we read (Acts 10:2) of Cornelius that he was "a religious man, and fearing God with all his house, giving much alms to the people and always praying to God." Then follows the account of the appearance of the

[1] *Summa*, IIa IIae, q.84, a.3 ad 3.

angel warning him to send to Peter. Similarly the corresponding vision of St. Peter: "And on the next day,
whilst they [the messengers of Cornelius] were going
on their journey and drawing nigh to the city, Peter
went up to the higher parts of the house to pray about
the sixth hour. And being hungry, he was desirous to
taste somewhat. And as they were preparing, there
came upon him an ecstasy of mind." [2] According to
St. Gregory's description, St. Benedict's vision also
was preceded by prayer. Mystical teachers speak of
the "prayer of rapture." They regard rapture as a
higher grade in the life of prayer. We are thus faced
with the task of clarifying the relation between prayer
and mysticism. [3]

In his *Summa theologica*, St. Thomas proposes the
question, whether it is becoming to pray. In this question his intention is to harmonize human prayer of
petition with unalterable providence. Naturally he re-
jects the view that God's foresight and decree can be
changed by our prayer: rather he brings our prayer
into conformity with what divine providence has determined: "We pray, not that we may change the
divine disposition, but that we may impetrate that

[2] Acts 10:9 f. St. Ambrose, *De Spiritu Sancto*, II, 10, 103: "Nam
cum in oratione vidisset coelum apertum, et quattuor initiis ligatum
vas quoddam, tanquam linteum in quo erant omnia genera quad-
rupedum." According to St. Thomas, there is question here also of a
rapture (*De verit.*, q.13, a.2 ad9).

[3] On prayer, cf. Tillmann, *Das Gebet nach der Lehre der Heiligen*,
1894. Zimmermann, *Lehrbuch der Aszetik*, 1932, pp. 372 ff. On the
psychology of prayer, cf. Mager, *op. cit.*, pp. 150 ff.

which God has disposed to be fulfilled by our prayers; in other words, that by asking, men may deserve to receive what almighty God from eternity has disposed to give." [4] St. Thomas gives further a direct reason why we should pray: "We need to pray to God, not in order to make known to Him our needs or desires, but that we ourselves may be reminded of the necessity of having recourse to God's help in these matters." [5] "God bestows many things on us out of His liberality, even without our asking for them; but that He wishes to bestow certain things on us at our asking, is for the sake of our good, namely, that we may acquire confidence in having recourse to God, and that we may recognize in Him the Author of our goods." [6] Thus the chief scope of prayer is, according to St. Thomas, didactic. By means of prayer our relationship to God is to be established on a correct footing.

This view of prayer is certainly justified. Moreover, it has found its way into ascetical literature. Yet the question may be asked, if thus the whole meaning of Christian prayer is explained. The thoughts reproduced above might be applied, as far as they go, to non-

[4] *Summa*, IIa IIae, q.83, a.2. Thus we see that St. Thomas has in mind primarily the prayer of petition. This is true of his whole attitude to prayer. He explains it as an act of religion, since "all those things through which reverence is shown to God belong to religion. Now man shows reverence to God by means of prayer, in so far as he subjects himself to Him, and confesses that he needs Him as the Author of his goods" (*ibid.*, a.3).
[5] *Ibid.*, a.2 ad 1.
[6] *Ibid.*, ad 3.

Christian prayer equally well as to Christian prayer. Perhaps we can determine with greater accuracy what is meant by strictly Christian prayer.

In his question on prayer, St. Thomas quotes a series of traditional definitions which afford us a starting point. We note that Christian prayer betrays a mystical tendency from the very beginning. In a passage of Pseudo-Dionysius, we read: "It is above all useful to begin with prayer, in which we surrender ourselves to God and unite ourselves to Him." [7] In the case of this writer his definition has a polemical edge to it: we do not pray to draw down God to us; rather, God unites Himself to us in prayer. Already a mystical note is sounded: in prayer God lowers Himself to the soul. This is not surprising from the Areopagite. But St. John Damascene says: "Prayer is the ascent of the mind to God." [8] Since Joseph of the Holy Spirit this definition has become current in mysticism: "Mystae definiunt orationem per hoc quod sit elevatio mentis ad Deum." [9] In the Catholic Cathecism we are told: "Prayer is the pious raising of the soul to God." [10] In this last case the adjective "pious" makes it quite clear that there is no question of any sort of elevation to God. For earlier theology this was implied in the terms ἀνάβασις and

---

[7] De divin. nom., 3; MG, III, 680.

[8] "Oratio est ascensus mentis in Deum" (Fid. orth., III, 24. Cf. Nilus, De oratione, chap. 35; MG, LXXIX, 1173).

[9] Op. cit., II, 41.

[10] Tenth edition (1933), p. 58.

elevatio, which bear a typically mystical stamp.[11] "Ascent" signifies growth in perfection: he who will be perfect may not remain on the "plain" or dwell on the "hills"; he must climb the lofty and arduous "mountain." [12] The *elevatio mentis* on man's side is counterbalanced by a descent on the part of God. Only then is real prayer possible, when God is willing to be addressed and descends to man. This view points to the fact that from the outset Christian prayer is intrinsically related to mysticism. St. Gregory calls contemplation a mountain, up which we climb, down which the Lord descends.[13] Some confirmation of this is to be found in the way the degrees of mystical union are regarded by tradition as being at the same time degrees of prayer: there is mention of the prayer of ecstasy, rapture, etc.; the degrees are thus at once indications of the life of prayer.

We cannot introduce at this stage a distinction between private and liturgical prayer, and consider this intimate relationship to God as holding good only in the case of private prayer. The revelations of St. Gertrude show that liturgical prayer also can blossom forth into mysticism. In fact, the mystics themselves have made reference to the importance of the choir

[11] For ἀνάβασις, cf. St. Gregory of Nyssa, *In Cant. Cantic., Hom.* 5; A. Dieterich, *Mithrasliturgie*, pp. 254 f. *Elevari* is one of the terms associated with the "journey to heaven"; "mens supra semetipsam rapta in superna elevatur" (Richard of St. Victor, *praep. an.*, 82).

[12] Origen, *Num. Hom.*, 22.

[13] *Mor.*, V, 36.

office in common for their prayer-life. If they were in any degree remiss at public prayer, they were urged on to zeal by all sorts of warnings and trials.[14]

Prayer is direct and intimate intercourse with God. "Prayer is intercourse and conversation with God," says St. Gregory of Nyssa.[15] And St. John Chrysostom: "Mark what happiness is bestowed upon thee, what glory granted to thee in that thou dost hold converse in prayer with God, dost enjoy intercourse with Christ, dost express whatever wish thou wouldst, and dost request what pleaseth thee." [16] To this corresponds the definition given by St. Teresa: prayer is enjoying friendly intercourse with God.[17] Christian prayer is based precisely on our divine sonship. The Christian speaks to God as to his Father. Hence the title "Father" stands at the head of the prayer which

[14] H. Wilms, *Das Beten der Mystikerinnen*, 1916, pp. 46 f. It follows from what has been said previously about sacramental union with Christ that all prayer is fundamentally sacramental and to that extent liturgical as well.

[15] Προσευχὴ θεοῦ ὁμιλία. *Orat. Dom.*, I.

[16] St. Thomas, *Summa*, IIa IIae, q.83, a.2 ad3.

[17] Joseph a Spiritu Sancto, *op. cit.*, II, 41. Today this thought is not taken very seriously, as appears from Zimmermann's criticism of this definition: "Repeatedly since early times it has been said that prayer is speaking with God, intercourse, conversation with Him. Since, however, ordinarily God does not speak in the strict sense, and is experienced only rarely by the soul as 'answering' or 'conversing,' but hears prayer rather merely by His action, or answers it by awakening some thought in our soul under the influence of grace, and that too only after a long interval, normally conversation takes place in a purely metaphorical sense. Hence we should not allow ourselves to be depressed by this definition." For him the definition ἀνάβασις νοῦ πρὸς θεόν is "an absolutely general expression" (*op. cit.*, p. 374 note 24).

Christ Himself has taught us. "In acknowledging God, the Lord of all, with our voice as Father, we signify that we have been summoned from the condition of servitude to that of sonship." [18] This filial relation gives us freedom of speech in regard to God: we now dare to call God our Father. Both these properties of Christian prayer (its intrinsic relationship to mystical union and its filial attitude toward God) spring from the same root, the friendship and sonship granted us through Christ. Christian prayer can therefore be made only in and through Christ, who alone is the way to the Father and our Mediator. If he who prays overlooks this, his filial converse with the Father is rendered a lifeless formula, or else it is paralyzed into silence before the majesty of God.

The freedom of speech which we have won toward God is manifested particularly in the prayer of petition for ourselves and for others, an essential element of Christian prayer. Hence the strong reaction on the part of the Church to the quietistic proposition of Michael Molinos: "It is not becoming for one who is resigned to the divine will to make any request of God: because petition is an imperfection, being an act of self-will and choice; it is to will that the divine will should conform to ours, not ours to that of God; and the Gospel phrase 'Ask and you shall receive' was not spoken by Christ for interior souls, who do not want

[18] Cassian, Coll., 9, 18.

to have any self-will; in fact, such souls have reached the stage when they cannot ask anything of God." [19] The rejection of this proposition implies that even the mystic, not having so far attained his final perfection, can address petitions to God (thus Zahn, *op. cit.*, p. 178), and that petitions for oneself and for others are essentially imbedded in Christian prayer. Thus we find petitions in St. Gertrude, even in her *Ambassadors of Divine Love*, in the midst of her highest mystical experiences. Moreover, St. Paul himself says that, in spite of his rapture into paradise he besought the Lord three times to remove the sting from his flesh. We can now understand why St. Thomas considered prayer so much from the point of view of petition.

The infallible effectiveness of Christian prayer is based on union with Christ: "If you ask the Father anything in My name, He will give it to you" (John 16:23). The prayer must be made in the name of Jesus, that is, in union with Him. Then it cannot remain unheard. St. Augustine explains this with incomparable beauty: "What is He called who has promised so great a grace? Christ Jesus. Christ means king, and Jesus means savior. Therefore not any sort of king will rescue us, but a king and a savior. Whatever we ask in opposition to our salvation, we do not ask in the name of the Savior. Yet He is our Savior, not only when He grants our request, but even when He does not do so.

---

[19] Denzinger: *Enchiridion symbolorum*, no. 1234.

When He sees that we are asking for something contrary to our salvation, by His non-bestowal He reveals Himself all the more as our Savior." [20] Because it rests on union with Christ, itself the basis of the mystical life, Christian prayer is essentially mystical prayer. But every Christian who prays is not thereby a mystic. Here the same distinction is forced upon us as was made in reference to oneness with Christ as the ultimate foundation of mysticism. The simple believer lets matters rest where they are, without developing that union to its full extent. For him prayer also is merely the fulfilment of an obligation, a good work which he performs like other good works, that is, in so far as it is commanded and is necessary. The perfect Christian, who suffers the germ of divine union to grow and fructify and who presses forward toward experience of the divine, sees in prayer, precisely as personal intercourse with God, an apt means of promoting mystical union with Him.

Prayer is an ascent to God, an ascent intrinsically connected with mystical union with God. However, as we have seen, mystical life can be illustrated from the condition of the soul which returns to paradise after death. But return and ascent to paradise are realized, according to the view of tradition, only step by step.[21] Thus we have a division into successive stages

[20] *In Joannem.* tr. 73, no. 3.
[21] Origen, *Princip.*, III, 6, 8, 9.

in the mystical life and in prayer. Normally the soul acquires its perfection by more or less prolonged practice and delay in the individual stages, since it has to maintain all the time a struggle against fresh difficulties corresponding to its state. In fact, mystical writers have enumerated various degrees of prayer, and they insist repeatedly that in most cases the soul makes progress in union with God and in the life of prayer only step by step. These divisions are always imperfect and incomplete, not perhaps because in many instances they are the work of theologians who have not themselves experienced the higher states of prayer: the real difficulty lies in the fact that it is a question of a prayer which by its nature does not provide the requisites for human and natural ordering and classification. Hence it has been possible to make the assertion: "It would not be enough to say: So many mystics, so many attempts at classification. Rather should we say: So many individual works on mysticism, so many efforts at classification" (Zahn, *op. cit.*, p. 261). In this place, consequently, we cannot enumerate all the attempts nor do we wish to increase them by still another attempt. It must suffice to present a few of them in an endeavor to detect from them the properties of mystical union. In so doing a clear distinction is to be made between the divisions from the time previous to Spanish mysticism and those of later date.

The mystical treatise of the Middle Ages, *De septem*

gradibus contemplationis (cf. Zahn, p. 261), reckons, as its title makes plain, seven degrees of prayer: fire, unction, ecstasy, contemplation (*speculatio*), taste (*gustus*), quiet, glory. "To begin with, the soul is inflamed when it is inflamed, anointed when it is anointed (*rapt*); in rapture it considers or contemplates; in contemplation it tastes; in tasting, it rests. All this the soul can attain in this life, not indeed immediately, but step by step. He who is more frequently exercised in spiritual things experiences this the sooner. The seventh degree will belong in fuller measure in heaven to those who have exercised themselves in the previous degrees." Of course this enumeration is not intended to retail a number of degrees in the life of prayer sharply marked off from one another, to be traversed successively by the soul until the beatific vision is reached. The essential idea behind it is that Christian life and Christian prayer are directed toward a spiritual tasting of the divine and a rest in it, the measure of heavenly happiness being determined by the degree of tasting reached upon earth. The number seven has been selected in view of the plenitude of the gift of the Spirit which unfolds itself in mystical life, not with the intention of marking out just so many stages in mystical life. The same holds good of other ancient reckonings, for example, when, probably in allusion to Exodus 3:18, three steps in contemplation are enumerated, because God instructed the people through Moses to

journey three days into the wilderness, and there to
sacrifice to Him. Others distinguish six steps, in reference to the six steps of Solomon's throne (III Kings
10:19). These divisions are the outcome of a purely
theological attitude; they are intended to give a definite significance to the whole process of striving
toward mystical union; the wandering in the desert is
the exit of the mystic from the world which is opposed
to God (an idea contained also in the theological concept of rapture); the mounting of the steps of Solomon's throne signifies the mystical life as an ascent into
heaven (Solomon's throne is an image of the heavenly
throne), or as growth in true wisdom. This theological
interest was bound to go beyond the triple division,
traditional especially since Pseudo-Dionysius: purga-
tive way, illuminative way, unitive way, since this
division finds its ultimate basis philosophically in the
threefold gradation in all temporal happenings (beginning, middle, end), and is thus less suitable for reproducing the special theological significance of the
mystical life.

With Spanish mysticism a new epoch dawns for
this division into degrees. It has been said that St. Teresa's particular merit is that she has provided a scientific definition of the degrees of contemplation
against which no objection can be raised. Poulain, too,
is of the opinion that through her an emergence from

the traditional vagueness was first effected.[22] Certainly
St. Teresa has given us a description and division of
the degrees of prayer worthy of the highest consideration. But that hers is the best or the only scientific and
unobjectionable division can be granted only if a preponderantly psychological standpoint toward mysticism is adopted. Her division is completely dominated
by psychological interest. Her aim is to mark off from
one another forms of prayer which signify a succes-
sion of degrees in the mystical life capable of being
experienced psychologically. In this her treatment is
essentially distinct from the earlier divisions into degrees, to which this standard may not be applied, psychological interest being quite remote from them.

To illustrate the several degrees of prayer, St. Teresa avails herself of the image of a castle with various
"mansions." The castle is the soul, the surroundings of
the castle are the body. In the mystical life the soul enters "into itself" until finally it reaches the last and
most beautiful chamber where intimate intercourse between the soul and God is enacted. In this St. Teresa
stands on the sure ground of tradition. The "entry
into the chamber of the heart" is an idea familiar in
mysticism. St. Gregory the Great speaks of the castle
of contemplation.[23] The number seven also rests on

[22] Poulain, op. cit., p. 540.
[23] E. g., Mor., VI, 37, 59. "Qui igitur culmen apprehendere per-

the older tradition, which St. Teresa retains in so far
as she prefixes three preparatory degrees to the four
which are strictly mystical. The mystical life, therefore, does not begin until a soul reaches the fourth
"mansion."

The fourth mansion is the prayer of quiet. According to Poulain, the name is selected because of the impression which the soul here experiences. "You are
suddenly taken possession of by an unaccustomed state
of recollection which you cannot help noticing. You
are overtaken by a divine wave which penetrates you.
You remain motionless under the influence of the
sweet impression. And then it all vanishes with equal
suddenness. Beginners feel surprised at this, for they
find themselves seized by an action the nature of which
they do not entirely understand. But they yield themselves to this inclination." [24]

According to Poulain, on the basis of the ten characteristics of mystical experience enumerated by him
(chap. 7, no. 11), it is not particularly difficult to establish whether a person has really attained to mystical
union. The prayer of quiet calls for a special attitude
on the part of the soul such as is not yet to be detected
in simple contemplation. For "we are confronted in
mysticism with a special form of life distinct from nor-

---

fectionis nituntur, cum contemplationis arcem tenere desiderant." St.
Teresa's immediate sources for *The Interior Castle* are discussed by
G. Etchegoyen in *L'amour divin*, 1923, pp. 333 f.

[24] Poulain, *op. cit.*, pp. 220 ff.

mal Christian life in the same way as the inanimate world is distinct from the animate." [25]

The fifth mansion designates for St. Teresa the "prayer of union." To distinguish it from the previous one, Poulain calls this degree the "complete or half-ecstatic union" in which the soul experiences no disturbances of any sort. It is called half-ecstatic because in this condition not every contact with the external world is broken off: the praying subject can still with more or less effort speak, walk, or terminate his prayer at will.

The sixth mansion is called the "ecstatic union." Here ecstasy makes its entry. The contact of the senses with the external world is broken off. The praying person can no longer move freely or cease from prayer; he has entirely "gone out of himself" and has been seized by God. St. Paul's rapture would belong to this degree; species of ecstatic union are reckoned as simple ecstasy when the separation from sense-life occurs gradually, and as rapture when this separation is introduced with violent suddenness. St. Teresa distinguishes further the "flight of the spirit," which causes the impression that body and soul have been separated.

The seventh and highest degree consists in transforming union with God, the deifying union or mystical marriage. This brings about a union of the soul with God which is the highest possible in this life. The

[25] Mager, *Mystik als Lehre und Leben*, p. 68.

individual feels himself closely embraced by the Person of the Godhead and in a certain sense one with Him.

These four degrees of mystical union are clearly constructed and sharply distinguished from one another according to the experience of union with God psychologically verified at the moment. A certain doubt can arise only in connection with the sixth mansion, the ecstatic union: for, as Father Mager rightly insists, ecstasies and visions are found, according to St. Teresa, in all degrees of mystical union, in this one, it is true, with a certain regularity, as a preparation for the transforming union; but the introduction of ecstasy cannot by itself constitute a strictly new degree of mystical union.[26] The degrees clearly distinguishable from one another would thus be reduced to three: the prayer of quiet, the prayer of union, and spiritual marriage.

This general survey shows how emphatically the degrees of prayer are divided from a psychological standpoint. Yet it is noticeable that the old nomenclature for the degrees has survived. Quiet, union, ecstasy are expressions which originally suggested a preponderantly theological meaning, without immediate reference to any specific psychological experience.[27] The theological meaning of these terms has

[26] *Ibid.*, p. 107.
[27] Butler has shown this very well for St. Gregory the Great in particular (*op. cit.*, pp. 122 ff.). Even Lieblang has to admit that

yielded place to their psychological signification. Obviously this does not mean that the prayer of "quiet" involves no sort of psychological perception of quietude, still less that these special psychological states enumerated by the later mystics do not exist. On the contrary, they occur in fact very often under regular conditions. But these terms did not acquire this special psychological meaning until the time of Spanish mysticism.

This fact is particularly significant, for example, in the case of the prayer of quiet. A remark of the Benedictine monk Benedict Schram (*circa* 1700) gives the right clue to the original meaning of this phrase. In his *Institutiones theologicae mysticae* (§284) he says: "The prayer of quiet is given various names by the mystics. It is called . . . quiet of the soul . . . prayer of darkness . . . sleep, death, the grave." The last term is common in St. Gregory the Great for contemplation. But for him there is no question of naming a definite degree of prayer in the sense of more recent mysticism. For St. Gregory the soul descends in contemplation into the quiet of the grave, in so far as it dies to the noisy life of the world. "The grave is the place in which the body is hidden. In like manner divine contemplation is a grave for the spirit, in which the soul hides. To a certain extent we are still living in

Gregory does not use the word "ecstasy" in reference to the condition known to us as ecstasy, and that he makes mention only once of what we understand today by ecstasy. Cf. *op. cit.*, p. 175.

this world, so long as we traverse it outside with our spirit. We shall be dead and hidden in the grave when, mortified in exterior things, we hide ourselves in the stillness of interior contemplation. . . . Thus he who seeks death rejoices when he finds the grave; so too he who intends to mortify himself will be glad to discover the quietude of contemplation." [28] "The grave can signify not only contemplation in this life, but also the quiet of the everlasting interior reward." [29]

Here contemplation is described as a quietude and as a grave, not, as in the case of St. Teresa and the moderns, on the grounds of a unique psychological experience, but in contrast to the multiplicity and distracted nature of worldly thoughts. This quiet is a mystical dying, a descending into the grave. Contemplation consequently is regarded in its theological sense in opposition to the distractions of secular life. Reference has been made above to the relationship of *apatheia* and *quies* in the sense of St. Gregory.[30] The "quiet of contemplation" will surely therefore be experienced as a liberation from the disturbing influence of passions and external things. On the other hand, there is no suggestion that the prayer of quiet is bound up with a special psychological state, such as is not yet realized

[28] *Mor.*, V, 6.
[29] *Mor.*, VI, 37. On the idea of quietude as part of the consummation of the life to come, cf. also Niederhuber, *Die Eschatologie des hl. Ambrosius*, 1907, pp. 79 f.
[30] Cf. *supra*, p. 91.

in "contemplation." In spite of this, we may reasonably speak of "quiet" as a special degree, in fact, as the first degree in the life of prayer. St. Gregory also describes liberation from the "noise" of thoughts and external occupations as a prerequisite for the quiet of contemplation.[31] Whoever is making serious efforts in the spiritual life will experience this quiet as soon as he begins to free himself from the disturbing influence of external things and from dependence on what is merely natural. Quiet is always the first stage and necessary condition of further advance in union with God. This quiet often can and does possess the characteristics enumerated by the more recent mystics. But that this is necessarily so, cannot be deduced from the concept of the older mystics. Once quiet has been gained, the soul is elevated to the divine vision: then this latter can be considered in its further development from angles that are theologically more positive.

This stage leads to the prayer of union. Here, too, we are dealing with a theological concept by which contemplation is explained theologically as union with Christ and as an expression of the marriage relationship between the soul and Christ. From this theological attitude we can understand why no special degree of "ecstatic union" is indicated in the earlier mystical writings. Ecstasy as a psychological experience is in general not valued very highly. Its theological signifi-

[31] *Mor.*, IV, 30.

cance appears especially from what we have said about the rapture of St. Paul out of the cosmos dominated by sin. Of psychological ecstasy St. Gregory merely remarks: "Often the spirit of the just is so suspended in the contemplation of higher things that their countenance externally appears to be paralyzed. But because heretics do not know that this power of contemplation works secretly, they believe that this occurs to the just and to men who are truly wise rather by some deception than in actual fact, because they are jealous that what they themselves cannot obtain should really be present in others." [32] Although Gregory is acquainted with the terms used in mysticism today to describe special psychological conditions, such as *raptus* and *extasis*, with him they allow of no reference to special psycho-physical phenomena. "All such psycho-physical phenomena were outside of St. Gregory's horizon." [33] When St. Gregory says that a man "is lifted out of himself" by contemplation, he is not describing some special happening specifically distinct from the normal life of the soul. He who has freed himself from external things and has attained to quiet, no longer lives in this world. "*Extra mundum esse*" and "*oratio ecstatica*" are, therefore, the stages following logically on quiet; in them man is able to occupy himself without hindrance with higher and heavenly

[32] *Mor.*, XII, 30, 35.
[33] Butler, *op. cit.*, p. 125.

things. At the same time the experiences described by modern mysticism may manifest themselves as indications of ecstatic union: yet earlier mystical literature does not put the principal emphasis on these latter.

This is shown, for example, by the way St. Gregory contrasts the sin of the prodigal son with the experience of St. Peter when the latter was freed from prison: "There are two ways in which we can be taken out of ourselves. Either we sink below ourselves through lowly thoughts, or we are raised above ourselves by the grace of contemplation. Thus he who kept the swine sank below himself by his dissolute and unclean thoughts; whereas he whom the angel set free and whose spirit was transformed in rapture, was indeed out of himself, but raised above himself. Both returned to themselves, the former by turning toward his heart again from his sinful works, the latter by reverting from the height of contemplation to the usual thoughts in which he had been occupied previously." [34] The return of the prodigal son to himself and that of St. Peter can be quite well understood without supposing any previous essentially distinct activity on the part of the soul in the state of sin and in contemplation; especially as Gregory in other places understands this being raised above oneself merely of the transcendence of the object of con-

[34] *Dial.*, II, 3.

templation. Lieblang is therefore justified in saying
that the "other regions" in which, according to St.
Gregory, a person moves in contemplation, are the regions of the supernatural, into which such a one is
raised by grace, and upon which his whole being is
focused in and by contemplation.[35]

The same can often be said of the notion current in
earlier mysticism. Even the highest degree of the mystical life in the sense of St. Teresa's division, the "mystical marriage" or "transfiguring union," bears a name
with a preponderantly theological meaning. Viewed
from the psychological aspect of later mysticism, the
expression "transforming union" is more suitable
(Poulain, p. 283) since it more accurately describes
the psychological result of this condition of prayer.
Transforming union implies an enduring union with
God, clear and lasting knowledge of God's presence:
further, a transformation of the higher faculties of the
soul. "The soul is aware that in the supernatural acts
of her intellect, her love or her will, she participates
in the divine life. . . . This is the essential part of the
spiritual marriage" (Poulain, p. 287). Finally a steady
vision of the most holy Trinity is added as belonging
to the mystical marriage. This is the final stage in mystical evolution, toward which, therefore, the entire
mystical life converges. Particular theological value

[35] Lieblang, *op. cit.*, pp. 135 f. This "life in the regions of the
supernatural" can, as we have explained in the chapter on the Dominion of the Devil, be connected with a transposition in place.

attaches to the fact that this condition is described by an expression familiar to us from the universally accepted doctrine of the Church on grace. For mysticism belongs to the Church and to Christian life.

According to Butler (p. 161) this meaning of "spiritual marriage" became current in the West through St. Bernard. But it goes back to the early idea of marriage mysticism. The Church is the bride of Christ, according to the patristic notion, because faithful and trustful surrender to God, longing for the possession of the good things of the next world, godlike behavior toward one's neighbor inspired by charity, are the response to the bestowal of grace by God, separating the Christian community from the world, proclaiming its state of spiritual virginity and its espousals with God. What holds good of the Church in general, can be said also of individual souls, since in them the Church is realized. Every soul, in virtue of its sacramental union with Christ, is a spouse of Christ. In the language of mysticism, the relationship of espousals becomes one of marriage. Thereby it is asserted that in mysticism it finds its supreme development. Moreover, in the case of the mystic there is added the "experience" of union with Christ. Thus it makes good sense to speak of spiritual marriage in mysticism, and there is meaning also in describing this degree of the mystical life as the highest. Once the passions have been quieted and the soul is completely immune from worldly influences, the experience of interior union with Christ can make itself felt.

From the above we can see in what sense mysticism and prayer are intrinsically connected. Christian prayer in its foundations is mystical so far as it proceeds from union with Christ. But every praying believer is not yet on that account a mystic. The intrinsic connection justifies us in speaking of degrees of prayer, since the mystical life is undoubtedly capable of development. In early theology the degrees of prayer are named from a preponderantly theological point of view: they are an attempt to give to mystical prayer-life as a whole a theological significance, and to depict progress in the spiritual life correspondingly. The work *Scala claustralium* or *Scala paradisi*,[36] composed about 1150, adopts possibly a middle position. According to this writer, contemplation has four degrees, upon which the soul "raises itself from earth to heaven": *lectio, meditatio, oratio, contemplatio*. The first three are directed toward the fourth. In reading, the matter is acquired; meditation loses itself in it; in prayer the soul turns to God that it may experience Him in contemplation. In the highest degree man is completely spiritualized, his flesh no longer resisting the spirit. "Happy is he whose spirit, free from all other occupations, is always intent to pass its time in these

---

[36] ML, CLXXXIV, 475–84. As to the author, cf. Wilmart, *Auteurs spirituels et textes dévots*, 1932, pp. 230 ff.

four steps." But, since a man cannot support the divine light for long, he must descend from contemplation to one of the lower steps, and exercise himself, now in one, now in another. On the fourth step the soul is "above itself," raised "right up to heaven," and thus attains to the highest mystical union. This can be understood as referring to a special psychological condition, but it can also be interpreted in the theological sense of St. Gregory as explained above.

Modern mysticism sees in the degrees of mystical prayer primarily special psychological manifestations of the mystical life, distinct from one another. Thus a uniform gradation is rendered both possible and necessary. For this outlook the enumeration of degrees of prayer given by St. Teresa has become classical. But even in this primarily psychological consideration of the degrees of prayer the old theological names have survived, nor should their theological meaning be overlooked.

The changed attitude toward the degrees of prayer reveals wherein modern, especially Spanish, mysticism is distinguished from earlier mysticism: it explains mystical terms, hitherto primarily theological in meaning, in a more psychological sense, thus leading to a preponderantly psychological consideration of the whole mystical problem. This consequence is seen most clearly in the description of the mystical experience. In saying this, we are raising no objection to

Spanish mysticism, which has a perfect right to adopt its own viewpoint and its own terminology. To the investigation of special psychological reactions in the mystical life, it has made a contribution not to be underestimated. But this fact should not be understood as though purely psychological standpoints embraced the essence of Christian mysticism in its completeness. On the contrary, its essentials lie beyond the psychological, and are not to be discovered from some particular spiritual state.

VIII

THE UNUTTERABLE WORDS

SO FAR we have spoken of mystical union under general headings. We have seen that the mystic knows God in a higher manner and experiences His presence. This knowledge and this experience of God must now be defined more accurately. Once again St. Paul's account of his rapture provides us with a convenient angle of approach.

St. Paul speaks of "visions" and "revelations of the Lord" bestowed upon him (II Cor. 12:1). He heard "secret words which it is not granted to man to utter." He does not tell us what he saw and heard. His polemical attitude toward his opponents, who overestimated such special revelations, may have been the factor determining his silence. In any case, to speak of them had no direct bearing on the salvation of the community. Even in other epistles he did not remedy this omission. Long ago Eusebius expressed surprise that Paul, so skilled in talking and so well able to formulate his thoughts, left behind nothing but short letters, "although he had innumerable mysterious matters to communicate, for he had attained even unto the sights of the third heaven, had been carried to the very paradise of God, and had been deemed worthy to hear unspeakable utterances." [1] Surmises as to what Paul heard are futile. But the way he describes his intercourse with God is not without interest. In this connection some writers have observed that, in the religious feeling of Judaism, "seeing" plays a subordinate role. The essential thing is "hearing." Among the Greeks, "seeing" was given preference to "hearing"; but the converse is true in Old Testament Jewish piety, where "hearing" is preferred to "seeing." [2] Only in eschatology, at the end of time, is "hearing" transformed for the Jew into "seeing." This view is given expression in the prophetical utterances concerning eternity. "Now it is no longer 'Hear Israel,' but 'Lift up thine eyes and behold' " (*ibid.*). A similar preference of "hearing" to "seeing" is verified at the outset of Christian revelation. The hearing of the word of Jesus signifies the bestowal of salvation. Our Lord is tireless in employing parables to urge His listeners to hearken. In this case, too, seeing is reserved for

---

[1] *Hist. Eccles.*, III, xxiv 4.
[2] G. Kittel, *Die Religionsgeschichte und das Urchristentum*, p. 100. In Judaism even prophetic vision is rather a veiling than a vision of God. E. Fascher, "Deus invisibilis," in *Marburger theol. Studien*, 1931, pp. 51 f.

eternity: "Blessed are the pure of heart, for they shall see God." This vision is bestowed upon the martyr Stephen at the moment of his martyrdom as he passed over to the other world. Kittel believes he can establish that, since the death of Jesus and His resurrection, seeing ranks equally with hearing. This is meant to imply that these happenings are already understood as being events in another world, as a dawning of eternity and the actualization of the divine proximity. Whether he is right or not, in any case it is no mere accident when in St. Paul's rapture the hearing of unutterable words plays a prominent part. Thereby the Apostle indicates that his experience is still bound up with "hearing," and was consequently neither supreme nor final.

According to a traditional opinion, Paul in his rapture was granted a fleeting but immediate vision of God. Therefore his experience signified the highest possible intimacy with God. St. Thomas mentions also another view, which considers that Paul did not see God directly, but saw only a reflection of His glory. St. Thomas, who favors the former opinion, appeals to the fact that the Apostle heard unspeakable words during the rapture. This fact seems to him to signify that there was question of the vision, since no eye has seen or ear heard and no mouth can express what God has prepared for His elect. Also in the case of Moses' celebrated meeting with God on Mount Sinai, St. Thomas admits a vision of God. Thus the greatest doctor of the Jews and the greatest doctor of the Gentiles were accorded this extraordinary grace.[3] Whether or not Paul in his rapture enjoyed the vision, is hard, if not impossible, to decide.

In its incomprehensibility, whatever St. Paul experienced is generally typical of mystical union with God. It is fundamentally something ineffable, something that cannot be rendered adequately by natural means of expression. It seems to imply an immediate contact with God, yet it retains something of the obscurity of faith. Consequently, even a theology of mysticism cannot satisfactorily explain the mystical knowledge and experience of God; such an attempt would be contradictory to their nature. At the most, their theological foundations can be indicated, and certain lines of demarcation laid down.

We spoke of knowledge and experience of God.[4] Actually, as regards mystical union with God, two questions must be distinguished. The first, so prominent in modern discussions on mysticism, runs thus: In mysticism is there any immediate, even if obscure,

[3] *Summa*, IIa IIae, q. 175, a. 3. Cf., on the whole question, Butler, *op. cit.*, pp. lxii ff.

[4] That in mysticism both knowing and experiencing play their part is made clear by Gerson (d. 1429) when he says: "It is better to say perception than knowledge (*cognitio*), for the former is a general expression for all the spiritual faculties, for cognitive and appetitive powers alike. In any case it seems that nothing can be perceived without the cognitive faculty sharing in it." Cf. K. Richstätter, *Mystische Gebetsgnaden*, 1924, p. 198.

knowledge of God? Thus the question concerns mystical union with God in so far as this involves knowledge. The second question probes into the meaning of mystical experience: How is this to be understood in general? This last question as to the essence of mystical experience is hardly asked at all nowadays; the experience is interpreted a priori as being purely psychological. The answer to it is reserved for the subsequent chapter.

The possibility and the fact of an immediate knowledge of God in mysticism is repeatedly proclaimed with reference to the mystics' teaching about the spiritual senses. In fact, the entire mystical tradition speaks of a seeing, hearing, and touching the transcendent actuality of God. All five senses of corporeal life are introduced to make comprehensible what the soul perceives in mystical union. The need of representing this by a comparison with bodily sense perception seems to prove that the question is one of an immediate knowledge of God, just as the senses apprehend their object directly.[5] A classical exposition of this teaching on the spiritual senses is furnished by St. Anselm of Canterbury in his *Proslogion* (chap. 17). He

[5] There is no question of invoking the doctrine of the five mystical senses only for a perception, and not for a knowledge, of God. As Gerson observes, they merge into each other. If mystical union were not knowledge, the intellect could not be the organ for the ascent of the spirit, which it clearly is, for example, in Richard of St. Victor. J. Bernhart, *Die philosophische Mystik des Mittelalters*, 1922, p. 116.

says: "Thou dost still hide Thyself, O Lord, from my
soul in Thy light and Thy glory: therefore it lingers
still in its shadow and woe. It looks around, yet sees
not Thy beauty. It hearkens, and hears not Thy harmony. It smells, but perceives not Thy perfume. It
tastes, but enjoys not Thy pleasing taste. It feels, but
feels not Thy delicacy. For Thou, O Lord God, hast
all this within Thee, in an unutterable way proper to
Thyself: Thou hast bestowed it on the things Thou
hast created in some way corresponding to their sensi-
ble nature. But the senses of my soul are numbed: they
have grown insensible: they are dulled by the long
misery of sin."

What Anselm is here striving after, to apprehend
God with the senses of the soul, others claim to have
achieved. St. John of the Cross says of this knowledge of God: "And these lofty manifestations of
knowledge can come only to the soul that attains to
union with God, for they are themselves that union;
and to receive them is equivalent to a certain contact
with the Divinity which the soul experiences; and thus
it is God Himself who is perceived and tasted therein.
And, although He cannot be experienced manifestly
and clearly, as in glory, this touch of knowledge and
delight is nevertheless so sublime and profound that it
penetrates the substance of the soul . . . for such
kinds of knowledge savor of the divine essence and of

eternal life." [6] Relying on these testimonies to the spiritual senses, Poulain maintains the immediate knowledge of God in the mystical state: "During the union, when it is not too exalted, we are like a man placed beside one of his friends, in complete darkness and silence. He does not *see* him, therefore, he does not *hear* him; he only *feels* that he is there by the sense of touch, because he holds his hand in his own. And so he continues to think of him and to love him." [7] Thus, in Poulain's opinion, there occurs in the mystical life an immediate contact with God.

Later, when we come to speak of the graces of the cross, we shall show that the meaning of the doctrine of the spiritual senses is different in its origin. The fact remains, however, that many mystics believe they have had a direct apprehension of God.[8] Before we try to answer this question, we must explain more accurately the viewpoint from which the theologian should discuss these declarations of the mystics in which they claim an immediate knowledge of God.

The mystic gives an account of his experience or, at least, of what he believes he has experienced. From his knowledge of the soul's life, the psychologist will endeavor to explain this experience or, once it can be

[6] *The Ascent of Mount Carmel*, II, chap. 26 (English trans., *The Complete Works of St. John of the Cross*, 1934, I, 196).
[7] *Op. cit.*, p. 95.
[8] Richstätter, *op. cit.*, pp. 117 ff.

accepted as certain, to estimate its value for knowing the life of the soul. On the contrary, the theologian's task is to show what can be said on the question from a theological view. Perhaps the mystic gives his experience a false interpretation. In certain conditions theology is able to demonstrate that the mystic's interpretation cannot be accepted, since it is in contradiction to certainly established theses in theology. Or else the theologian will try to establish the possibility of the experience claimed, by pointing out the supernatural data on which it is based, and will endeavor to grasp its meaning. Thereby obviously no judgment is formed as to the reality of any individual mystical experience. That is not the theologian's concern. Since the mystics in almost unbroken array lay claim to an immediate knowledge of God, the reality of the experience seems highly probable, and the attempt to explain it is rendered the more urgent. Hence we must first deal with the question whether theological anthropology has room for an immediate knowledge of God. In the sense of a transient vision, this knowledge is certainly possible. But this possibility does not solve the problem at issue; for in most cases the mystics are concerned, not with the *visio*, but with knowledge of God which, though immediate, is nevertheless grounded on faith, and is thus obscure.

In works on mystical theology, which, after the style of Poulain, confine themselves to a presentation of the experiences and results of the mystical life, no mention is made of the essence of sanctifying grace, of the indwelling of God, etc. Others, dealing with the dogmatic bases of mysticism, do indeed presuppose such doctrine, or make mention of it in an introductory section (e. g., Tanquerey, *Précis de théologie ascétique et mystique*, 1924, pp. 56 ff.). Yet great importance attaches to the examination of these points in direct connection with the question of the mystical knowledge of God.

In this examination, it seems advisable to proceed from the standpoint of Scholastic theology, in an effort to extract from that source an answer to the question about the possibility of the immediate apprehension of God. In this endeavor the work of the Dominican, A. Gardeil, *La structure de l'âme et l'expérience mystique* (2d ed., 1927), furnishes us with foundations. According to Gardeil, in the soul of the justified are "two realities to be taken into account. There is God substantially present in the core of all things, and thus in the essence of the soul, by His presence of immensity. . . . But there is, furthermore, and this exclusively in the soul of the just, that radical power of grasping God intellectually, which we call sanctifying grace. Thus, in the very depth, in the essence, of the soul of the just, God offers Himself in an obscure manner, as the predestined object of knowledge and love, to the soul deified by grace. This immediate presence . . . of the divine object in the justified soul is actualized in mystic contemplation. . . . It finds its supreme realization and immediacy in mystical experience, strictly so-called" (I, xxiii). These data must be explained, and their value in furnishing and understanding mystical knowledge must be estimated. The following points call for separate discussion: the essence of sanctifying grace and of the supernatural state of grace in general, participation of the divine nature, the doctrine of the indwelling of God in the souls of the just, the doctrine of the state of grace as a beginning of eternal life.

1. The Essence of Sanctifying Grace

Significant for the entire teaching of St. Thomas on the supernatural life and the gifts of grace included in it, is his alliance with Aristotelian philosophy. There results from this, as regards the supernatural life, an attitude which in some particulars must have struck the guardians of traditional thought as a bold innovation. Aristotle, because of his naturalistic outlook, was sometimes looked upon by patristic theology as the father of all heresy.[9] He now provided the philosophical system to which Christian revelation contributed

[9] De Ghellinck, "Quelques appréciations de la dialectique d'Aristote durant les conflits trinitaires du IVᵉ siècle" in *Revue d'histoire ecclésiastique*, 1930, pp. 5–42. Faustinus writes in the fourth century against the Arians: "Ubi sunt nunc illa impia vestra sophismata, quae Aristotelis episcopi vestri magisterio didicistis?" (*Trin.*, 12.)

that very completion for which it was waiting. The dictum *gratia supponit naturam* seemed to be fulfilled in the most glorious way in the relation of Christian revelation to Aristotelian philosophy. "St. Thomas did not intend to show merely that the Greek could in the long run adapt himself to Christianity, but that in fact Christianity was necessary to him, that it alone fully safeguarded his ideal and could achieve its perfect realization. With its supernatural faith and its grace, Christianity fulfilled the longings of the Greek world, though this latter knew nothing of them, and scarcely dared hope for them." [10] The Thomistic-Aristotelian doctrine of grace may be outlined as follows.

St. Thomas contemplates man as a being who, by his very nature in ever progressing and freely self-determined development, is seeking his way to his final end. This final end is God. With the aid of Aristotelian philosophy, St. Thomas explains this thesis from the nature of the human will which is directed toward the good in general, not toward this or that particular good: hence it finds its complete satisfaction only when it has attained to the fountainhead of all goodness.[11] That God is man's final end and that we must strive toward Him, is established over and above this from revelation. Man's final union with God is, according to the principles of Aristotelian philosophy, to be

[10] E. Gilson, *Saint Thomas d'Aquin*, 1925, p. 6.
[11] *Summa*, Ia IIae, q.2, a.8.

found in the vision of God's essence. As a Greek, Aristotle recognizes in the intellectual vision the supreme happiness of man. That this vision must in the final instance penetrate to the essence of God follows from the nature of the intellect. In his persistent questioning as to the "why," man is led on always from one cause to another, until finally he encounters the first cause of all becoming. The intellect desires to know this too, and not merely the fact of its existence or its essence in some general way: the mind will be satisfied with nothing less than a clear and direct vision of the essence of the first cause, God.[12] The final end of man, therefore, is the possession of God in an immediate and undiluted vision of His essence. This philosophically established truth [13] receives its confirmation through revelation, which likewise promises for the future life a vision of God "face to face" (I Cor. 13:12).

The philosophical investigation leads still further. Although it shows that nothing but the immediate knowledge of God can give final satisfaction to man, yet it sees clearly that man alone, by the powers naturally at his disposal, can never reach this end. To know is after all to receive the being of another into oneself. Such knowledge is naturally always in pro-

[12] *Ibid.*, q.3, a.8.
[13] It has been much disputed whether in these reasonings St. Thomas really intended to abstract from revelation. We cannot enter into the question more closely here.

portion to the nature of the knowing subject, which
cannot receive within itself after the manner of knowledge something transcending its own natural mode of
being.[14] On these grounds no created knowing is capable by itself of an immediate reception of God's essence, since this latter infinitely transcends all natural
being. In a certain sense this thesis reproduces the
Catholic doctrine of the transcendence of the Christian's final end, and of man's incapacity, without the
intrinsic assistance of grace, to achieve his own sanctification. Here, then, is the place to insert the fact that
grace has actually been bestowed, a fact known only
from revelation. This fact is an article of faith and, in
contradistinction to the foregoing considerations, cannot be demonstrated from purely philosophical premises. Without the light of revelation man would have
had to resign himself to the realization that it would
never be possible for him to attain to his complete and
final happiness; that he would have to be content with
a lesser, imperfect happiness, such as corresponds to his
natural faculties, and in which he would not obtain an
immediate knowledge of God's essence, but only an
analogous knowledge about God from His activity in
creatures. Christian revelation alone gives the consol-
ing information that even man's ultimate aspiration is
to be satisfied and that his elevation to the state of grace

[14] "Si igitur modus essendi alicujus rei cognitae excedat modum
naturae cognoscentis, oportet quod cognitio illius rei sit supra naturam illius cognoscentis" (*Summa*, Ia, q. 12, a. 4).

insures for him the possibility of immediate knowledge
of God. It is here clearly evident how St. Thomas sees
in Christian revelation the fulfilment of natural capacity and desire.

In explaining also how the Christian approaches his
supernatural end step by step, St. Thomas makes extensive use of analogies from Aristotelian philosophy.
Man, unlike the pure spirits, does not possess his perfection in the first moment of his existence; he must
acquire it gradually.[15] Even to direct his activity
toward the new supernatural end in this life, his soul
needs a new entitative reality. He is not determined to
the supernatural end by a decision on God's part leaving man intrinsically untouched and unaltered. This
determination gives him even now a new being. If man
is determined to a new end transcending nature, this
implies a special love on the part of God. God's love
does not presuppose goodness in creatures, but creates
it. A special act of divine love creates therefore a special state of goodness also in the human soul, in our
case sanctifying grace. "Even when a man is said to be
in another's favor, it is understood that there is something in him pleasing to the other; even as anyone is
said to have God's grace; with this difference, that
what is pleasing to a man in another is presupposed to
his love, but whatever is pleasing to God in man is

[15] *Summa,* Ia IIae, q.5, a.7.

caused by the divine love." [16] With these considerations St. Thomas justifies from his theological system what revelation tells him by its doctrine of the re-creation or regeneration of man in holiness, namely, that a new being is bestowed upon the sanctified soul.

To define the nature of this new being, St. Thomas takes his stand on the principle that it is to be essentially helped in the effort toward the new supernatural end. Now God can give this assistance in two ways: first as a transitory support for individual acts of merit; or as a new, intrinsic, stable principle of activity, by means of which man can of himself, and, as it were, in accordance with his nature, perform acts in preparation for the supernatural end. St. Thomas decides in favor of the latter notion, and in so doing appeals to the analogy of the natural order, where each being receives as something stable the faculties it requires and is enabled by their means to operate in accordance with its nature. It would be unworthy of the order of super-nature, to be equipped in a less harmonious fashion.[17] The new state of grace is thus to be regarded as a stable perfection of the soul. Hence we can see how grace is visualized in the Thomistic system. It is something habitual, that is, a new being, produced by God's special love in the soul, enabling its possessor to perform

[16] *Ibid.*, q.110, a.1 ad1.
[17] *Ibid.*, a.2. Cf. Gardeil, *La structure de l'âme et l'expérience mystique*, 1927, I, 362.

in accordance with his nature meritorious works leading to the supernatural end of the immediate vision of
God. This notion of grace is fundamental in Thomistic
theology. It is developed quite justifiably from a single
idea, according to which the essence of the order of
grace implies the determination and the equipment by
means of which man can strive toward the possession
of God in immediate vision here on earth, and realize
it in the next life.

2. Participation of the Divine Nature

It is in the light of this basic idea in Scholastic theology that the second element of the supernatural life,
the participation of the divine nature, is to be understood. In an absolutely general sense, every creature
shares in the divine nature, in so far as, produced as it
is by God, it bears within itself a reference to its first
cause. However, when the tradition of the Church
speaks of a deification through grace, it means something substantially more. This deification of which
tradition speaks is realized by sanctifying grace and the
theological virtues: "For as a man in his intellective
powers participates in the divine knowledge through
the virtue of faith, and in his power of will through the
virtue of charity, so also in the nature of the soul he
participates in the divine nature, after the manner of
a likeness, through a certain regeneration or re-

creation." [18] In the view of St. Thomas this participation has a definite importance; it involves a power to direct oneself toward the divine essence, so as to make it the immediate object of the soul's faculties in their activity. According to Thomistic principles, no one can give effect to a spiritual activity unless he possesses the nature proportionate to such activity.[19] The brute animal cannot think, since it does not possess a rational nature. Now the whole meaning of man's elevation to the supernatural is to equip him so that he may be capable of acts which are natural only to God. He is to gaze at God face to face. If, therefore, St. Thomas deduces from this the necessity of an objective endowment of grace in the souls of the just, it is but a further step in the same process of thought when "sanctifying grace" is apprehended as being in its essence a participation in the divine nature. It is nothing else than the objective foundation in the interior of the soul for an activity in harmony with its nature in regard to acts which are of themselves divine.[20]

3. The Presence of God in the Soul of the Just

An understanding of the third supernatural element, the presence of God in the soul of the just, is also closely bound up with the Scholastic concept of

[18] *Summa*, Ia IIae, q.110, a.4.
[19] *De veritate*, q.27, a.2.
[20] Gardeil, *op. cit.*, I, 370 ff.

participation in the divine nature. According to St. Thomas, it transcends the divine omnipresence in created things: "God is in all things by His essence, power, and presence, according to His one common mode. . . . Above and beyond this common mode, however, is a special mode belonging to the rational creature wherein God is said to be present as the object known is in the knower, and the beloved is in the lover." [21] This teaching of St. Thomas has received widely different interpretations from his commentators. It is certainly not obvious as it stands. We must see whether and how God is essentially present to the soul in this new mode, especially as this new presence seems to have nothing at all to do with holiness. For cannot even a pagan philosopher or a sinner make God the object of his knowledge and love, and thus enjoy the second form of presence described by St. Thomas?

According to Vasquez (d. 1604) God is present only so far as He produces the creature by His power and conserves it in being. The distinction made by St. Thomas between the two modes of presence implies merely that, since grace is a particularly noble effect of God's activity, to that extent we can speak also of His special presence in the soul of the just. This presence in the soul of the just, because of the special operation itself, is also of a distinct and nobler kind. On the other hand, Suarez (d. 1617) declares that St.

[21] *Summa*, Ia, q.43, a.3.

Thomas must be understood as referring to two modes of presence, essentially distinct from each other. Consequently he distinguishes the presence of the first cause in its effects from that of the beloved in the lover. Love and friendship (grace brings about a relationship of friendship to God) tend to bring lover and beloved together. If, in spite of love and friendship, among men this being together is not always realized, this is due to the force of external circumstances. In the case of God such hindrances do not occur. Therefore, because of the status of friendship effected by grace, He will be present constantly to the sanctified soul. As a final conclusion, Suarez deduces from his concept that, supposing God's omnipresence came to an end, He would still be present always as a friend in the soul of the just. Both views, that of Vasquez and that of Suarez, are not without difficulties. In the case of Vasquez, it does not appear how a new mode of presence is brought about, such as St. Thomas wished to assert precisely for the sanctified soul in contrast to the general presence of God in all things. Suarez deduces very well the fact of a new presence, but neglects to explain it.

The famous Thomist, John of St. Thomas (d. 1644), endeavored to discover a middle way. He retains emphatically the essential distinction between the two presences, but says that the second necessarily supposes the first. With him the bearing of the doctrine of the presence of God on questions of mysticism is already apparent. According to him, God is present in the soul of the just as in all other things by His omnipresence. For a soul in the state of grace this presence is modified to the extent that now, thanks to the supernatural force of grace, God is present in it also as experimentally knowable and perceptible. Thus the new mode of existence consists in the fact that God, who is always present in the profundity of the soul, becomes now a direct object of knowledge, owing to the supernatural faculties which the subject of grace alone possesses, and which, as explained above, are characterized precisely by being immediately directed toward God.

This view seems to approach nearer than others to the thought of St. Thomas. But when it is said that God is present to the just like the object known to the knower and the beloved to the lover, it is not necessarily a matter of actual knowledge and love; otherwise, upon the cessation of these acts, the indwelling itself would terminate. If a man possesses the capacity for a definite knowledge, we are fully entitled to say that the object in question is habitually in his knowledge and love. In the believer God brings about a new capacity in the spheres of knowledge and love. In consequence of this, God is at the same time present as an object to be known immediately in His essence, that is, not merely as first cause. Thus John of St. Thomas is right in considering the indwelling in the just without abstracting from the omnipresence. He goes beyond the data provided by St. Thomas when, in this context, he speaks of an experimental knowledge. For the interpretation of St. Thomas and the Scholastic teaching on the presence of God in the soul, all that is necessary is the radical, potential, immediate knowledge of God furnished already in this life by the supernatural gifts of grace.

All three properties of the justified soul—its holiness, its participation in the divine nature, and the indwelling of God—are thus to be viewed in Thomistic theology from a single unifying standpoint, that of capacity for the immediate vision of God. This requires a new form of being in the soul, imparts a participation in the divine nature, and also explains the new presence of God. Herewith new actualities are provided for an immediate and intimate intercourse with God, realities which are wanting to the soul of the unsanctified.

4. The State of Grace as a Beginning of Eternal Life

Of themselves the three supernatural elements in the sanctified soul render the life of grace here on earth a beginning of eternal happiness. This concept of the mysterious commencement of everlasting life reproduces ancient theological tradition and describes exactly the nature of the eschatological time when earthly and other-worldly, divine being is fused into one. Here again the Aristotelian system furnishes a means of explanation.

In the life of grace the Christian is even now striving toward the immediate vision of God as his future end. To this striving may be applied the Aristotelian principles of entelechy and finality. In accordance with these principles, in the case of any striving toward an end, some actualization of that end in the person striving is necessarily presupposed. Obviously this conclusion does not imply that there must be an actualization of what is yet to be attained; but there must be a natural relationship between the striving subject and the end.[22]

The reason for this view is metaphysical. "A thing is desirable only in so far as it is perfect; for all desire their own perfection," says St. Thomas (*Summa*, Ia, q. 5, a. 1). In other words, every striving aims at perfecting the striving subject. When the question is one of perfection, the end must be the perfecting of a tendency already presupposed. Hence St. Thomas says that being directed toward an end is of itself a half-possession of the end, an *imperfecte habere*.[23] Man's capacity for aiming at a natural happiness by his own powers lies in this, that by his nature he has within

[22] For the following, cf. A. Stolz, O.S.B., *Glaubensgnade und Glaubenslicht nach Thomas von Aquin*, 1933, pp. 59 ff.
[23] *Summa*, Ia IIae, q. 16, a. 4.

himself potentialities which he brings to their full development by his own activity. (St. Thomas is here speaking as an Aristotelian philosopher who knows nothing of the existence of original sin, and for whom the non-realization of the supernatural end has nothing to do with man's loss of his proper end.) Hence, as far as the supernatural vision of God is concerned, its supernatural character consists precisely in this, that man's nature lacks such active potentialities as could themselves be developed without special extrinsic help so as to lead to the direct vision of God. The fact that we are at present directed toward that end and that we are aware of this in faith, calls for some actualization of the end, an *inchoatio vitae aeternae:* otherwise effectual striving toward the divine vision is impossible.

This beginning is actualized in us by the supernatural gifts of grace, by sanctifying grace in the very essence of the soul, and by the theological virtues of faith, hope, and charity in its faculties. We should here note that the beginning of eternal life in the intellect through faith does not as yet imply any insight into the mysteries of faith. Our present condition, in which the soul is united to the body, excludes this. The habit of faith is a beginning of the divine vision in a fashion of its own, without evidence and in mysterious obscurity. Accordingly, at the end of our earthly pilgrimage, the grace of faith as something imperfect must fade away and give place to the light of glory, which then gives us insight into what was hitherto accepted on faith.

This is what Thomistic theology understands by the supernatural life of grace. The Christian really begins a new life which, though surrounded and veiled by the visible and the natural, effects an obscure beginning of the next life with its immediate enjoyment of God.

The Thomistic explanation of the immediate knowledge of God in mysticism, as represented in recent times by Père Gardeil in particular, proceeds from a comparison between the supernatural data and the natural and immediate self-knowledge of the soul. According to this view, the human soul which receives within itself the supernatural life of grace is not merely the subject of, but also the pattern for whatever takes place in mystical knowledge. The reason for this parallelism is that God is essentially no less close to the soul and, because of this new life, not less within its reach than is the soul itself.

That the human soul in some way or other knows itself is an incontestable fact. For this to be so, philosophically speaking, three things are required: (1) a permanent, immediate, and intellectual self-awareness, equivalent to an experimental perception in potentiality; (2) any act of knowledge; (3) a reflection on this act of knowledge penetrating to its root, that is, to the soul itself in so far as it is the principle of this act (cf. Gardeil, II, 95 ff.).

The first point is of fundamental importance. Without habitual and permanent self-awareness, equivalent to self-knowledge in potentiality, a man reflecting upon his act of thought would never arrive at the result: I think; but at the most to a result: There is thought going on, that is, someone is thinking. For the conclusion, I am thinking, a permanent intellectual self-awareness is required. It is called permanent or habitual in contrast to an actual and immediate self-awareness on the soul's part, which, as long as the soul remains united to the body, cannot be realized satisfactorily. In itself every spirit—and thus the human soul also—is perfectly knowable and perfectly capable of knowing itself. Hence in the spirit a permanent self-knowledge is realized by its natural power.

With the "pure spirit," that is, the angel or man's soul after its separation from the body, this self-knowledge is achieved immediately. But in the case of the human soul united to the body, such knowledge is impeded and to some extent suspended, since the soul in its knowing activity is now dependent upon the body and attains to itself only reflexively by the round-about route of sense objects. The permanent, habitual self-awareness mentioned above consists for the present in the fact that the soul possesses immediate self-knowledge in potentiality already, but this cannot be fully actualized. Even now a certain actualization takes place, as soon, namely, as any act of knowledge is elicited. Then at the same time a measure of self-knowledge is achieved, because the knowing subject possesses the other as something objective. "Even when the perceiving subject perceives an object, this subject, at least indirectly, perceives itself. To possess something as the object of perception is to perceive something as being distinct from the subject. Hence in the case of self-knowledge the perceiver perceives self as something objectively distinct." [24] If, therefore, the soul reflects on its knowledge and discovers itself as the actualized principle of this act, some degree of self-knowledge is achieved,[25] an experimental self-presence, which can be compared to direct sense knowledge. In this case the experience bears upon the actually existing being of the soul itself which is apprehended in some way as the conclusion of this self-analysis.

By analogy with this self-knowledge, Thomistic theology is able to understand the immediate mystical knowledge of God. God is present immediately and most intimately to the soul, namely, as the ultimate principle of the new supernatural equipment of grace. In exercising the supernatural virtues, the soul elicits

[24] Cf. J. Gredt, O.S.B., *Elementa philosophiae Aristotelico-Thomisticae* (1926), I, 361.
[25] Gardeil, *op. cit.*, II, p. 113.

acts corresponding to its supernatural being. A reflection upon the proper vital principle of this activity can, in a manner analogous to the soul's knowledge of itself, lead to an experimental perception of God operating in the soul, that is, to an immediate mystical knowledge of God. This knowledge is as immediate as is the corresponding self-knowledge of the soul. And there is a parallelism in so far as in both cases a complete apprehension of the object (the soul itself or God) is impossible in this life. "An immediate union between God and the soul, in the depths of the soul, has been established ever since the infusion of grace, and by this infusion and the uninterrupted vivifying of the sanctified soul by God, the soul has acquired the faculty of experiencing God, substantially present within it, vivifying it. And if at the infusion of grace the soul was that of an adult, it has been able to experience Him forthwith." [26]

In this explanation of mystical knowledge as paralleled by the soul's knowledge of itself, we are dealing with an analogy. In the natural order this knowledge must lead to an immediate self-knowledge even though this is obscure. In the supernatural order, because of the absence of evidence in the life of faith which must still go on developing, this necessity does not arise at the outset. It first occurs when the light of faith fades before the light of glory, and then the immediate

[26] *Ibid.*, p. 254.

union of God and the human soul is fully effected. By the comparison and the analysis of the structure of the soul, if one may use such an expression, only the possibility of an immediate knowledge of God is demonstrated. In other words, from the standpoint of Thomistic theology there is nothing contradictory in the assertion of the mystics that they have experienced an immediate knowledge of God.

The principal opponent of an immediate knowledge of God in mysticism is Saudreau. By his arguments he tries to prove that the immediate knowledge of God involves always the beatific vision. "Every creature that perceives God Himself not only knows Him as present, but also, since God's presence is not distinct from His attributes, sees that God is essentially simple, that His existence is identical with His essence, that His nature is one, that this nature is common to the three Persons distinct from one another, etc. In a word, the creature sees Him, as the theologians say, *totum, licet non totaliter.*[27] In the same place Saudreau protests against the notion of an immediate but obscure perception of God. To perceive God is to see Him, just as we can perceive light only when we see it.

This is correct inasmuch as the immediate knowledge of God never results in a vision in embryo (at the most in exceptional cases, such as St. Thomas admits for Moses and St. Paul). For that, the light of

[27] *L'état mystique,* 1921, p. 313.

glory would be required. But the immediacy of mystical knowing is not thus refuted. The knowledge of God as the mytics in general describe it rules out any vision. Immediate contact with God in His essence blinds the human knowing faculty. Thus the teaching of the mystics on the obscurity of mystical knowledge has a significance of its own. Obscurity is essentially associated with the immediacy of mystical knowledge. Just as the blazing light of the sun blinds the feeble human eye, so does the being of God blind human knowledge, though in mysticism this sometimes apprehends God directly. As long as the body and soul are united in this life, the divine light cannot but engender "darkness." [28]

As the conclusion of our inquiry into the immediate knowledge of God in mysticism, we may say that the mystical knowledge of God, of which the mystics frequently speak as of an immediate apprehension of God, does not necessarily include an immediate vision of the divine essence. A transitory, immediate vision of God might be possible even in this life as a miracle. St. Augustine and St. Thomas admit such a miracle in favor of the two great universal doctors of mankind, Moses and St. Paul. An immediate apprehension

---

[28] "This divine obscurity is not indeed due to absence of light; it implies rather excess of light on God's side, blinding the natural light of understanding, or that light connatural to it in this life." (The last words refer to the light of faith.) Vallgornera, *Theol. myst.*, I, 451. Cf. St. Anselm, *Proslogion*, chap. 16.

of God, even without any vision of the divine essence, can be acknowledged from a theological standpoint as possible.

With this conclusion, taking it strictly, we have acquired a merely apologetical, not a theological, insight into the question. A claim made by the mystics has been defended and shown to be not devoid of possibility.

IX

MYSTICAL EXPERIENCE

UNDOUBTEDLY St. Paul's rapture meant for him a quite extraordinary psychological experience; so much so that he was unable even to state whether he was in the body or taken out of the body into paradise. Is not every mystical experience, not merely such an extraordinary case as this, bound up with a special psychological condition? Earlier authors, in treating of contemplation, do not invariably make mention of such psychological reactions. Hence the objection has been made against St. Thomas that in his theological system there is no room for an explanation of mystical knowledge: it is said that he never in any form raised the question about the specific nature of the mystical state. "The precepts of Aquinas were not sufficient to determine in any satisfactory scientific manner the specific nature of the mystical state. On the contrary it can be shown that the saint either failed altogether to recognize the mystical state as something distinctive in the soul or, at any rate, deemed it unworthy of a scientific investigation." [1] This objection is the more surprising since St. Thomas discusses the problems of contemplation in the closest dependency on the master of mysticism for the Middle Ages, St. Gregory the Great (*Summa*, IIa IIae, q. 180). The objection is understandable to some extent if we admit that modern theorists in mysticism, when they are treating of the nature of the mystical state, have a different outlook from that of St. Thomas and his master, St. Gregory. In such circumstances it can easily come about that sufficient value is not attached to St. Thomas's treatment of the question.

Mystical union with God implies essentially an experience of the divine. On this point early and modern mysticism are in agreement. The only question is how is this experience to be understood. As illustrated by the quotation just given, it is regarded today in many cases from a purely psychological point of view. In these circumstances to speak of a mystical state is to have in mind an experience of the divine which is bound up with just such a special condition on the part of the soul. Since St. Thomas, like many older mystics, hardly mentions any such special condition, we may surmise that in fact he represents a different

[1] "Der hl. Thomas und die Mystik" in *Theologie und Glaube*, 1921, p. 7.

attitude toward mystical experience. This will now be demonstrated.

As we have already insisted more than once, the doctrine of grace in the Western Church is under the dominant influence of the psychological viewpoint. This fact will explain how it is precisely modern Western mysticism that has come to insist so much upon the psychological element in mystical life, and why, in so doing, it disregarded theories of the past upon which St. Thomas, in spite of his Scholastic outlook, which was not exclusively psychological, has bestowed his loyal approval. Hence our inquiry may well start from the standpoint of the pre-Augustinian doctrine of grace, to see what interpretation of mystical experience may be forthcoming from that angle of approach.

The essential distinction between the Scholastic and the earlier patristic concept of the nature of grace may perhaps be reduced to the following formula: Scholastic theology, chiefly under the direction of Aristotelianism, and its attitude to the problem of God in relationship to the world, in harmony with this system, regards the influencing of the creature by God as an effect accomplished by an efficient cause.[2] Earlier theology, on the other hand, considers rather the formal cause, that is, God in so far as He

---

[2] M. J. Congar, "La déification dans la tradition spirituelle de l'Orient" in *La vie spirituelle,* 1935, pp. 99 ff.

communicates being—an expression of the conviction widely spread in early speculation that the divine world is not only exemplar and efficient principle for the formation of this universe, but at the same time its intrinsic ontological foundation, reaching down into earthly things and determining the formal basis of their being.

As it is expounded by this view, created being is a participation of the divine being, although in an imperfect and attenuated form. This concept is neither pantheistic nor monistic. Again and again the early theologians emphasize in clear-cut terms the essential distinction between the earthly order, sharing in being, and the divine order, dispensing being. A classical instance is the proof of the divinity of the Holy Ghost. According to the testimony of Scripture, the Holy Spirit bestows on us Christians a participation in holiness. Therefore He Himself does not belong to the order of those who receive participated being, to the order of creatures, but to the order of those who dispense being: He is God. Thus the difference in essence between God and creature is deliberately stressed. In this view the perfection of a thing will consist in its realizing more and more the divine idea by which it is intrinsically determined in its being. Perfection implies being informed by the divine being in the highest measure. If the state of grace is a participation in God's being, then its goal must be a restoration of deified humanity. This restoration is a recovery, by means of grace, of the "essential likeness" to God which has been lost, or defaced, because of sin. The ontological being of man must be brought to its full development.

Later Western theology has preferred to speak of the holiness which is to be acquired by the agency of the new faculties bestowed in grace. The goal of holiness is no longer regarded primarily from the angle of a restoration of the image of God, likeness to God, but from that of an activity to be realized, the direct vision of the divine essence. This is the fundamental reason why the sum total of Christian teaching is regarded by each theology from a different angle. The earlier, ontological, attitude values the work of redemption more from the physical factor, that is, as sanctifying and transforming; the other, viewing it from the standpoint of the capability thereby recovered of performing actions pleasing to God, is forced into adopting a more ethical and juridical conception. A similar distinction is found in their manner of conceiving the Church. The pre-Augustinian theology contemplates it preferably from the sacramental point of view as communion in holiness and thus as the society of the saints. Post-Augustinian theology regards the Church rather as the society of combatants (*ecclesia militans*), an organized society, ensuring us of greater relief in the struggle for the highest good. This struggle entails naturally a different concept of man. It brings into opposition a more ontological estimate of man and a more ethical and moral anthropology, the latter finding its chief expression in the idea of supernatural merit (in contrast to deification and ontological sanctification). Consequently we must form a more exact notion of this preference for the ontological which in older theology dominates the concept of sanctification by grace, so that, taking it as our starting point, we may arrive at the meaning of mystical experience. For this an explanation of the ideas of likeness to God and the garb of holiness is particularly helpful.

What proceeds from God and depends upon Him shares in some way in His being. Hence man, owing to his natural dependence on God, resembles Him, shares in His nature; he is the son of God. This is not to confuse the order of nature with that of grace. The doctrine of image (*imago*) and resemblance (*similitudo*) emphasizes the distinction between them. The image implies the natural likeness to God; the resemblance, the supernatural. This likeness to God can be obscured and concealed by sin, but can never be obliterated entirely. The perfect image of God is His only begotten Son, to whom man, who is called to perfect likeness unto God and to sonship in grace, must be conformed. Because of his rational nature, man participates already in the nature of the second divine Person, who is the Word and Knowledge (*Logos*) of the Father.[3] This likeness to God obtains its supernatural redintegration by the sacrament of regeneration. Baptism restores to its primitive luster the image disfigured by original sin. With the sacrament of baptism the likeness to God, in common with Christian being in its entirety, is bestowed as something capable of development. By dint of personal effort (of course, under the influence of divine grace), man must perfect within himself the image of God. Thus the image admits of degrees and steps in perfection. But always it is primarily conceived, not dynamically as an activity, similar in form to that of God, but ontologically as a determination of being, although one which admits of further advance.

A similar notion of the state of grace is presupposed by the concept of the "robe of holiness." Even today we still speak of the robe of sanctifying grace and of the staining of this robe by sin. For us, however, the expression is hardly more than a metaphor: for the older theology it has a special value. This rests on the different estimate of garb in general. According to the older notion, dress is more than an outward sign. It bestows the dignity which it indicates. The garment

---

[3] "The image of God is His Word, the genuine Son of Mind is the divine Word, the archetypal light of light; and the image of the Word is the true man, the mind which is in man, who is therefore said to have been made in the image and likeness of God" (Clement of Alexandria, *Protrepticus*, 10).

makes its wearer in human society what it represents. This thought lies at the bottom of the saying: Clothes make the man. The "theology of dress" is based on this idea.[4] Thus is explained the significant part played by dress in the ancient mysteries. Here holy vesture makes a man holy. This estimate of clothing occurs also in the Christian Church. St. Paul's exhortations to "put on" Christ and to "put off" the old man, suggesting at once the picture of a garment, presuppose this attitude toward dress. The same idea is expressed also in the symbolism of monastic garb. For centuries the reception of the monastic habit was regarded as equivalent to profession. It has been disputed why in earlier times monastic novices never received the habit of the order. The reason is evident if we recall the ancient attitude toward dress. By receiving the habit, the novice would have become a professed monk.[5]

The garment of holiness has another special meaning in the tradition of the Church: it is the vesture of light. By this is expressed the participation in the divine nature which is bestowed with the new garment of grace.[6] If, therefore, the state of grace is regarded as a reception of a garment of light, thereby is indicated

[4] E. Peterson, "Theologie des Kleides" in *Bened. Monatschr.*, 1934, pp. 347–56.
[5] St. Benedict received the monastic habit from the monk Romanus ("eique sanctae conversationis habitum tradidit," *ML*, LXVI, 128), and was reckoned as a monk thenceforward.
[6] Cf. Bäumker, *Witelo, ein Philosoph und Naturforscher des 13. Jahrhunderts*, 1908, pp. 357 ff.

the ontological perfecting of the sanctified soul to a godlike degree, and its elevation into the sphere of the divine. Thus the two anthropological ideas of pre-Augustinian theology meet: participation in the divine and the garment of holiness. Both give expression to the fundamental notion of the sanctification of man by grace: a penetration in the order of being, effected by the divine nature, which raises man above his nature into a higher, divine order. The difference between this and the basis of the Scholastic idea is clear: in the former view, the accent falls upon the new godlike being; in the latter, on the capability of godlike activity.

From this newly gained basis let us try to reach the meaning of mystical grace in the sense of the older theology. Evidently in this connection another outlook is possible besides that presupposed by modern theorists in mysticism. According to this older view, it is not obvious that a special state of soul is necessarily bound up with this mystical grace which is an intensifying of the ordinary grace of justification. That such a state can arise and frequently does so, is an indisputable fact, but perhaps there is a stage at which the essentials of mystical experience are present without these being necessarily attached to a function of the soul proper to themselves.

From the standpoint of the pre-Augustinian doctrine of grace, mystical life appears as an intensifica-

tion of simple Christian life, and at the same time as
an intensified self-determination brought about by
divine ordering. The development of the grace of
justification, common to all the faithful, into mystical
life in the sense of the older doctrine of grace can best
be seen in its concept of "divine birth." [7] The state of
grace gives divine being, divine life. The life of God
is revealed in the eternal birth of the Logos. Hence
that divine life bestowed in baptism is also a Logos-
birth. It is the Logos "who is being born ever anew
in the hearts of the saints." [8] But the work of sanctification is not thereby concluded. The growth of
baptismal grace in the believer is a growing up of
Christ within the Christian: it is perfected by a constantly increasing knowledge of the divine truth.[9] It
is perfectly comprehensible when St. Gregory of
Nyssa defines mystical perfection, founded on the
grace of baptism, as a birth of the Word in the believer. He says: "The child born to us is Jesus, who
grows up differently in wisdom, age, and grace in
those who accept Him. He is not the same in all. For
according to the degree of grace in him whom He
informs and according as the receiver is capable of it,

[7] H. Rahner, "Die Gottesgeburt. Die Lehre der Kirchenväter von
der Geburt Christi im Herzen des Gläubigen" in *Zeitschr. f. kath.
Theol.*, 1935, pp. 333 ff.

[8] *Epistula ad Diognetum*, XI, 3.

[9] "Propter nos et in nobis ipse dicitur proficere; sic enim refertur
quia: Jesus proficiebat aetate et sapientia apud Deum et homines"
(Origen, *Cant. Cantic.*, *Prolog.* Cf. Rahner, *op. cit.*, p. 363).

He appears either as a child, an adolescent, or a fully developed adult." [10] The same thought is reflected by Maximus Confessor (d. 662), for whom the birth of the Logos is realized perfectly in the mystic.[11]

In this view mystical life is understood as the harmonious evolution of baptismal grace. It is the perfect Logos-birth in the believer. In its beginnings and in its first growth, the divine life, although substantially supernatural, is not bound up with some special psychological state in the faithful specifically distinct from their normal spiritual activity. Therefore the interpretation of mystical life as completing what has taken place at baptism does not indicate that mysticism begins only when the human soul functions no longer as informing the body but as a pure spirit. There is no hint that the experience of God, which is the distinctive characteristic of mystical life, is necessarily to be associated with something "entirely new" in the course of the soul's life, as maintained hitherto.

This truth can be presented also in the later theological terminology influenced by Aristotelian philosophy.

By the justification and regeneration of baptism, a seed of supernatural life has been planted in the soul of the believer. The seed must grow and eventually

[10] *In Cant. Cantic.*, 4.
[11] Rahner, *op. cit.*, quotations on pp. 376 ff.

determine the whole being of the individual. This compenetration is accomplished in so far as his spiritual existence, enshrining his likeness to God, is seized upon and transformed by the principle of supernatural life. The first transformation of our spiritual existence, as far as the faculty of knowledge is concerned, we describe as the virtue of faith. This virtue, which is infused into the soul along with sanctifying grace and the other gifts in the process of justification, raises our knowing powers to the higher, divine order. This information by faith, like the entire life of grace, is also capable of growth. The distinction made long ago by the Alexandrian theologians between simple believers and those who have deeper insight expresses that sufficiently. The mere believer is satisfied simply to accept supernatural truth. With a tranquil certitude, by the intrinsic light of faith, that is, the deification of the intellect, he gives his assent to dogmas. The virtue of supernatural faith is simultaneously a light furnishing him with certain knowledge that in revelation the word of God is brought to him. The ontological completion of his knowing faculty through faith not only inclines him to assent to the articles of faith, just as he gives his assent to other well attested events in history; it provides him over and above this with a spontaneous, and in a certain sense baffling, explanation of the divine character of the articles of faith revealed directly to his "deified" intellect. As

St. Thomas points out, it is a question of a *judicium per modum inclinationis*, in contrast to the *judicium per modum cognitionis* of rational, discursive knowledge.[12]

We are here touching the root of the theological concept of the supernatural character of faith. The act of faith is for every believer something going beyond an assent psychologically explainable; it is an act by which the subject accepts higher first principles of knowledge, an acceptance which later on, under the influence of divine grace, is to widen out into the immediate vision of God as the consummation of this superior form of knowledge. Already, therefore, for the grace of faith there exists a possibility of growth and further expansion, in so far as the knowledge conditioned by it approaches more perfectly the consummation of the divine vision.[13]

The likeness to God, which every gift of grace, and thus the virtue of faith, brings with it, is a relationship to the world of the divine, a relationship that grows as the state of grace intensifies. As the habit of faith develops, it gives more profundity to the supernatural knowledge in which the believer gains insight into the divine character of the contents of faith. The

[12] *Summa*, Ia, q.1, a.6 ad 3.
[13] "Denique quoniam inter fidem et speciem intellectum, quem in vita capimus, esse medium intelligo, quanto aliquis ad illum proficit, tanto eum appropinquare speciei (ad quem omnes anhelamus) existimo" (St. Anselm, *De fide trin*).

believer does not merely see that the truth is of God
and that he ought to believe it: his knowledge advances farther along this plane and becomes a gazing
(obscure, owing to the non-evidence of faith), and
understanding, a tasting: in short, it develops into
an experience of the divine truth.[14] To some extent
the believer sees already the contours of what he is
later to contemplate in an open and unveiled manner.
At this stage, in the teaching of the older theology,
the simple believer becomes theologian, gnostic, and
mystic. The absolute obscurity of faith is not penetrated, but the deified intellect gains deeper and more
immediate insight into revealed truth, not by way of
logical knowledge and deduction, but by means of its
own deified being, which permits it to lay immediate
hold on supernatural truth.

For determining the nature of mystical contemplation, fundamentally significant is the fact that the
root of this intensified knowledge lies beyond the
psychological sphere. Hence the essence of supernatural faith, the deification of our spiritual existence,
and the vision of the divine in revealed truths which
it effects, is not bound up with a special psychological
happening. As far as structure is concerned, the
spiritual activity of the believer assenting to revela-

[14] St. Gregory, *Mor.*, XXX, chap. 19, no. 64: "Montes pascuae sunt
altae contemplationes internae refectionis. Sancti enim viri quanto
magis se exterius despiciendo dejiciunt, tanto amplius interius con-
templatione pascuntur."

tion is not distinct from a natural act of the so-called *fides scientifica* which rests on a natural perception of credibility. However, this latter in its essence is infinitely distinct from a supernatural act of faith, for this enshrines a supernatural vision springing from the deified being of the knowing faculty. But in this way the new vision and tasting of the truth which deepens the insight common to all believers is not structurally different from similar activities, and in its essence is not outside the boundaries of what can be established in a purely psychological manner. It is not always and necessarily demonstrable in the psychological sphere as a different action and reaction on the part of our intellectual faculties. In this sense mystical experience can be described by a rather paradoxical expression as "transpsychological" experience.

But this expression is not meant to assert that mystical experience occurs entirely and completely beyond the psychological sphere: that would be in last resort to deny its nature as an experience, and would be paralleled by refusing to admit the supernatural act of faith as an assent. Just as the act of faith, considered as an assent, does not manifest any difference in psychological structure from natural acts of assent, but is nevertheless essentially distinct ontologically from them, so mystical experience, though not necessarily bound up with a special state of soul, possesses none the less its special being, the presence of which, like that of supernatural faith, cannot be established psychologically.[15] Of course any sort of knowledge through faith with emotional reactions, such as any believer may have, is not therewith mystical experience. For this latter an intensified seeing is required, arising from the knowledge provided by the light of faith. And no one asserts that mystical experience never admits of a special activity of soul. In proportion to the psychological dispositions of the individual believer, in proportion to the intensity of the mystical experience, or in conjunction with a special gift of divine grace, mystical experience will produce also its special psychological effect. This may manifest a regularity conditioned by the natural equality which holds good for man. The regularity of this special activity of soul in the case of individual mystical experiences has been observed and investigated since the time of Spanish mysticism. But we must regard this special psychological condition as the essence of mysticism, or affirm that, apart from it, a mystical experience is inconceivable. To do so would be tantamount to demanding a special state of soul for an act of supernatural faith.

[15] The supernatural believer knows that he possesses supernatural faith: even so is the mystic, too, aware of his mystical experience. Nevertheless he does not always verify its presence from the fact that it is a psychological *novum* in the course of his soul's activity, no more than the believer does so in the case of his faith.

The special psychological state with which mystical experience can be associated is possible even in non-Christian religions, once religious life has reached a certain pitch, and indeed in philosophical speculation. It is comparable to the condition of a Christian mystic, and can display equivalence or similarity in its psychological structure. The essential nucleus, however, of mystical experience, like supernatural faith itself, is to be found only in Christianity. It is a false deduction to conclude from the similarity of psychological phenomena in Christian and non-Christian piety to the existence of true mysticism outside Christianity. Since the essence of mystical experience lies beyond the psychological plane, neither can it be explained and set forth by purely natural means of expression, or by a description of psychological states. The essential factor in mystical experience remains ineffable, baffling explanation. All attempts to set forth mystical life must in the end content themselves with the acknowledgment made by St. Paul that there were unspeakable words which it is not given to man to utter.

After what has been said, we may now answer the question which had to be left open at the close of the second chapter. We said that the question whether mystical life corresponded to the normal and necessary completeness of Christian perfection depended upon whether a special psychological state belonged to the essence of mysticism. We have since reached the conclusion that such a special condition is not necessary. There is thus no difficulty in conceiving mystical life as the normal rounding off of Christian perfection. He who remains in this life bound to a simple faith of assent and does not develop the supernatural life in general and the life of faith in particular, that is, who does not become a mystic, has, in the place of purgation after death, still to make up what the mystic reaches in this life, perhaps without experiencing any psychological reaction of a special kind in so doing.

We progressed to our knowledge of mystical experience in its essence from the pre-Augustinian doctrine of grace as our starting point. From this angle of approach we could the more easily recognize the higher evolution of faith in mystical experience as an intensified self-determination by means of the supernatural, which does not necessarily reach as far as certain frontiers inside the area of psychological happenings. This view has survived even in Scholasticism. This comes to the fore more clearly in connection with the doctrine of the gifts of the Holy Ghost.

X

THE PLENITUDE OF THE SPIRIT

WHILE investigating the dogmatic foundations of mystical knowledge of God, we made no special reference to the gifts of the Holy Ghost. A theology of mysticism, however, cannot entirely overlook them: the role of the Holy Spirit in mysticism is too important to permit of that. For it is the Spirit who throws open to us again the approach to paradise; [1] He it is who does battle for us against the demons; [2] He teaches us the ineffable, that which man may not utter, the description of which is beyond the human tongue.[3] Furthermore, the connection between prayer and mysticism, of which mention has been made, calls for a special consideration of the activity of the Holy Ghost. Christian prayer is undoubtedly

[1] "Once a fiery sword barred the entrance to Paradise; a fiery, beneficent tongue brought salvation back again" (St. Cyril of Jerusalem, *Cat.* XVII, 15).

[2] *Ibid.*, 19.

[3] Origen, *Princ.*, II, 7, 4.

due to the Spirit of God: "for we know not what we should pray for as we ought; but the Spirit Himself asketh for us with unspeakable groanings" (Rom. 8:26). Our task will be first to give a brief exposition of the doctrine of the gifts of the Holy Ghost and their relation to mystical life according to the mind of St. Thomas; then to show the basis of this teaching in revelation, and thus discover its theological meaning and its significance for mysticism.

In Scholastic theology the doctrine of the gifts of the Holy Ghost has been built up in a way which very often leaves the modern reader with the impression of something subjective and unproved. Yet at the basis of the doctrine is much that comes from tradition.

St. Thomas introduces it as supplementary to his teaching on the supernatural virtues (*Summa*, Ia IIae, q. 68, a. 2). He regards the *dona* as supernatural and habitual gifts of grace distinct from the virtues. Emanating from sanctifying grace, the supernatural virtues lay the foundations in us for godlike activity and meritorious striving toward the supernatural end. Yet they contain a certain imperfection. To bring this fact into prominence, St. Thomas starts with a consideration of the supernatural equipment needed by man on his way to the new end beyond nature. The infused virtues of faith, hope, and charity form the operative principles of supernatural life. Since, how-

ever, these are received in human faculties, they are
to some extent subordinated to rational knowledge
and function according to that purely natural mode of
activity lying within man's powers. Their operation
does not as yet proceed exclusively according to the
divine norm.

In order to remedy this defect, the gifts are su-
peradded. These render man receptive and docile, so
that he hearkens to the inspirations of the Holy Spirit
and acts in accordance with their impulse. Thus, absolutely speaking, supernatural activity does occur prior
to the gifts. Even a person in mortal sin, who has lost
charity and along with it the gifts of the Holy Ghost,
can elicit a true act of supernatural faith. But, "with
only the virtues, even though they are supernatural,
man is like an apprentice who knows fairly well what
he must do, but who has not the skill to do it in a
suitable manner. Consequently the master must come
from time to time, take his hand, and direct it so that
the work may be presentable." [4] In the virtues, supernatural conduct accommodates itself to our faculties.
In accordance with the rules of prudence and under
the direction of our reason illuminated by faith, always
of course under the influence of divine grace, we take
the initiative. "By means of the gifts, God acts in a
supra-human way. He Himself takes the initiative.
Before we have the time to reflect and consult the

[4] Garrigou-Lagrange: *op. cit.*, p. 282.

dictates of prudence, He sends us divine intuitions, lights and inspirations which act in us, without deliberation on our part but never without our consent." [5]

The difference between acting by means of the virtues and by means of the gifts in an individual instance may be illustrated thus: faced with a difficult decision, the supernatural virtue of prudence takes into consideration all the circumstances, pondering over them and weighing them against each other; the gift of counsel, on the other hand, makes everything clear in an instant. "In a difficult situation, where two duties in apparent opposition must be harmonized, prudence is, as it were, perplexed; it hesitates, for example, about what answer to give so as to avoid a lie and keep a secret. In certain cases only an inspiration of the gift of counsel will enable us to find the proper reply without in any way failing in the truth, and without having recourse to mental restrictions of dubious morality." [6] Not unjustly is the man who acts by force of a supernatural virtue likened to an oarsman who strikes out on his own initiative, whereas the man who acts by reason of the gifts of the Spirit resembles a sailor who, drifting before the wind, is subject to a higher force and advances with greater speed.

[5] Tanquerey, *The Spiritual Life*, 1932, p. 610.
[6] Garrigou-Lagrange, *op. cit.*, p. 277.

From the above we see that activity by means of the gifts becomes more constant and more intense as the soul grows in perfection. Only in such activity is Christian conduct perfected. It would be wrong for a Christian, in impetuous striving toward perfection, to desire to surrender himself completely at the outset to the inspiration of the Holy Ghost and the operation of the gifts. In fact, no one can correctly interpret the impulses of the Spirit and obey them until, by persistent and persevering practice of virtue, he has died to the deceptions of self-love, of pride, and of the flesh.

In enumerating the individual gifts of the Holy Ghost, Scholastic theology takes as a basis the well-known text from the prophet Isaias in which it is said of the Messias that the Spirit of God will rest upon Him: "The spirit of wisdom and of understanding, the spirit of counsel and of fortitude, the spirit of knowledge and of godliness. And . . . the spirit of the fear of the Lord" (11:2 f.). Since the gifts of the Holy Ghost perfect man's operations in the Christian sense, these seven gifts are divided among the corresponding three theological and four moral virtues. This results in the following "supernatural organism," as Garrigou-Lagrange terms it.

The gifts of understanding and knowledge correspond to supernatural faith (*Summa*, IIa IIae, q. 8 f.). They perfect the simple assent of faith and allow of a more profound penetration into revealed truth. The gift of understanding does this after the manner of an intuitive contemplation of divine things. The gift of knowledge does not bestow this intuitive apprehension of the objects of faith, but rather the power of discernment, to distinguish what is to be believed from what is not to be believed.

Hope is supplemented by the gift of divine fear; not as though the Christian by means of this gift lived in fear that God, upon whom he has built his hope, is going to desert him. Rather he is afraid, in view of his own weakness, that he may himself withdraw from God's help. Thus hope and fear are intrinsically connected (*Summa*, IIa IIae, q. 19, a. 9 ad 1um).

On the virtue of charity is erected the gift of wisdom. For the mystic this gift is of supreme importance. Charity gives a natural affinity to God: from this emanates the gift by which everything is estimated from God's viewpoint. St. Thomas makes this clear by an example: "Thus, about matters of chastity, a man after inquiring with his reason forms a right judgment, if he has learnt the science of morals, while he who has the habit of chastity judges of such matters by a kind of connaturality. Accordingly it belongs to the wisdom that is an intellectual virtue to pronounce judgment about divine things after reason has made its inquiry, but it belongs to wisdom as a gift of the Holy Ghost to judge aright about them on account of connaturality with them" (*Summa*, IIa IIae, q. 45, a. 2). The gift of wisdom is thus the instinct springing from affinity to God enabling us to judge correctly in matters pertaining to Him.

The gift of counsel follows on the virtue of prudence. By divine inspiration it supplies what human consideration cannot attain (*Summa*, IIa IIae, q. 52, a. 2).

The virtue of justice reveals its supreme activity in divine worship. The gift of piety corresponds to it. This begets a childlike awe toward anything connected with God and the worship due to Him (*Summa*, IIa IIae, q. 121, a. 1).

The gift of fortitude pertains to the virtue of that name. It implants in man the strength not to leave off the good, no matter how many difficulties may confront him. "It surpasses human nature to attain the end of each work begun and avoid whatever perils may threaten" (*ibid.*, q. 139, a. 1). Above all, the gift of fortitude gives an increase of confidence.

It will be seen from this summary that the gifts are invariably concerned with perfecting in a supernatural direction that which lies within the scope of the bare virtue.

The doctrine of the gifts of the Holy Ghost in general is, even if only indirectly, linked up with mysticism by the theologians. The mere presence of the gifts does not, indeed, make the mystic, but of their very nature they render the soul receptive to the impulses of the Holy Spirit. Certain gifts, namely, those of understanding and wisdom, have a direct reference to contemplation, in so far as they sharpen the vision for the objects of faith. Since, according to the teaching of St. Thomas, the gifts in the case of every believer are necessary for salvation, without them a perfect Christian striving, essentially impelled by the Holy Ghost, is impossible. They are operative even before the entry of mystical contemplation, and thus, in simple prayer and meditation, they prepare the way for mystical graces. The special gift of grace which must be claimed as the immediate principle of mystical life is the gift of wisdom. This bestows a relish for supernatural truth in God and a vision of it. Since wisdom rests on an affinity to the divine, it grows with charity. Hence it is this gift, grounded as it is on charity, which St. Thomas connects with the famous quotation from Pseudo-Dionysius, in which the latter speaks of "sympathy with" divine things: "Hierotheus is perfect in divine things, for he not only learns, but is patient of, divine things."

"Now this sympathy or connaturality for divine things is the result of charity, which unites us to God" (*Summa*, IIa IIae, q. 45, a. 2). In this knowledge, therefore, charity plays a special part. It not only impels the intellect to apply itself in general to divine things; it seems to transform the object itself, which,

now that it is connatural to the knowing subject, takes
on a new guise. Charity steers the mind beyond all
that can be pictured by the imagination or represented
by the intellect. To know God, not in any purely conceptual manner, but, as it were, in experimental fashion, as He is in His inmost life, in His proper essence,
in His divine being, that is what is meant by tasting
God through the gift of wisdom. St. Thomas speaks
of this "tasting" contemplation, following here in the
footsteps of tradition, especially in those of St. Gregory the Great (*ibid.*, q. 180). In this life contemplation does not reach to an immediate and clear vision
of God, unless perhaps in a transient manner, as in
the case of St. Paul (art. 5). Contemplation gives rise
to a special delight because it is occupied with the
object of supernatural love. How firmly, according
to St. Thomas, contemplation is rooted in charity
appears from the fact that contemplation itself lasts
as long as charity is present: the contemplative life
is said to remain by reason of charity, wherein it
has both its beginning and its end (art. 8). St. Thomas
makes this assertion in spite of the clear testimonies
of such a one as St. Gregory the Great, according to
which, here on earth, the human mind cannot for long
immerse itself in contemplation, because it is dazzled
in the brilliance of the divine light.

With unimportant differences this doctrine of the
gifts of the Holy Ghost is common to Scholastic the-

ologians. In its reference to mysticism we can see the direct connection with what was said in the last chapter. There is no hint in St. Thomas to the effect that he associates the connatural tasting and experiencing of divine truth by means of the gifts of the Holy Ghost with a special psychological happening. On the contrary, for him it is nothing more than the normal continuation of that seeing and knowing which grace confers on every believer in the act of faith. This is because for him the question of contemplation is one of a knowing built on affinity in essence to the divine, just like the illumination induced by the grace of faith. In his later works, he divides among the grace of faith and the individual gifts several functions, including the tasting of the truth, which in earlier works he ascribes to the habit of faith.[7] What the gifts of the Holy Ghost provide is, therefore, in no sense rendered accessible by a special state on the part of the soul. Thus we have no warrant for reading into St. Thomas the view that mystical experience is invariably associated with a special psychological occurrence. For him mystical life is already present, even when no special activity of soul can be observed. Of course this does not mean that he regards such activity as impossible, but that with true theological sense, like St. Gregory, he pays no particular heed to it.

The doctrine of the gifts of the Holy Ghost, espe-

[7] Stolz, *Glaubensgnade,* p. 92.

cially when considered in its basis in revelation, puts mystical life before us from new points of view.

The text of Isaias (11:2) from which the Scholastics derive the sevenfold number of the gifts of the Holy Ghost, forms, in its original context, part of the so-called "Gospel of Prophecy." What is deduced from it in the first place is that Christ possesses the fulness of the gifts of the Holy Ghost, and that He bestows these gifts, as being His own, upon the faithful.[8] Furthermore, the text is employed as a proof of the two natures, human and divine, in Christ. Thus we are dealing here with a Messianic text, that is, a prophecy describing the way the Redeemer and the redeemed are endowed with grace. The text is hardly applicable as a proof of the nature of the gifts as distinct from the virtues.[9] The sevenfold number enters in only as being the number of perfection and of plenitude. Tradition itself understands the gifts in general after the fashion of the Scholastic virtues, as helps in the struggle toward perfection and sanctity.

In Christ there is concentrated the plenitude of all these graces and of the activity of the Holy Ghost. The anthropological significance of this fact is that the whole treasury of Christ's grace is bestowed upon

---

[8] Schlütz, *Isaias 11, 2* (*Die sieben Gaben des Hl. Geistes*) *in den ersten vier christlichen Jahrhunderten*, 1932, p. 148.

[9] According to Mitterer, the gifts as regarded by the fathers have a similarity with the nine charismata; they are perhaps actually identical with the virtues.

the faithful through the gifts of the Holy Ghost. In
mystical perfection, consequently, we are concerned
with an assimilation to Christ through the Spirit.
Here is indicated already the role of the individual
divine Persons in mystical life—a matter to be discussed in detail later. If Scholasticism identifies the
plenitude of graces merited by Christ with the gifts
of mystical contemplation, theologically this can mean
only that the fulness of Christian being, Christian life
in its strict and real sense, seeks to express itself in
these gifts of grace. It implies also that every Christian
is called to put into practice what these gifts are intended to bestow.

We must observe further that the Messianic plenitude is connected with the eschatological outpouring
of the Spirit. Of this latter St. Peter speaks in his first
Pentecost sermon: "These are not drunk, as you suppose. . . . But this is that which was spoken of by
the prophet Joel: And it shall come to pass, in the
last days, saith the Lord, I will pour out my Spirit
upon all flesh, and your sons and your daughters shall
prophesy" (Acts 2:15 ff.). Mystical life and prayer,
as operations of the eschatological Spirit, are the
earnest money of fulfilment; they are the pledge and
commencement of that intercourse and of that union
with God which consummation entails. Understood
in this eschatological aspect, Christian mysticism and

Christian prayer cannot be compared with non-Christian phenomena.

The question may be asked why it has come about precisely in Scholastic theology that the gifts of the Holy Ghost should have obtained this significance as supplementary to the virtues. A hint is to be found in the remarks of St. Thomas and of the later Scholastics, when they speak of the incompleteness of the supernatural virtues. The supernatural equipment of grace, with which man is supplied, consists, in St. Thomas' view, in a sort of duplication of the apparatus of virtues, which itself rests on a duplication, that is, an elevation, of our final end: to the natural end, the analogical knowledge of God, accedes the supernatural, the immediate vision of God. The new end postulates a new being. Thus in the supernatural sphere the being of grace corresponds to natural existence; the infused virtues, on the other hand, correspond to the natural faculties. The regulative principle of the natural order receives its completion in the reason guided and illumined by faith.

This view no doubt has its advantages, especially for illustrating positively in what relationship nature and grace, considered ontologically, stand in regard to each other. But the danger is not far remote of conceiving the supernatural order of grace in too naturalistic a fashion. For this very reason, in its early period, the Thomistic system was received with suspicion: it has forced its way only gradually to the recognition granted it today. In fact, there is the temptation to see in the supernatural and in the grace of Christ nothing more than that completion which is missing from the Aristotelian picture of the world. This temptation is vanquished if we see, along with St. Thomas, in the supernatural life of the virtues merely an *aliqualiter* and *imperfectum* of the life of grace. Although they do, along with sanctifying grace, constitute the essence of the supernatural, yet they are to some extent "naturalized." In their activity they depend indeed upon reason illuminated by faith, yet it is reason still upon which they continue to depend.

To go no farther than this, would be to form a completely false idea of Christian life. Christian life is not merely life in accordance with reason; it is life in accordance with higher, super-rational, divine, standards. Fully to Christianize the Thomistic picture of man, the gifts, as principles of a higher activity, are on this account unavoidably necessary. They make it possible for a permanent principle directly controlling Christian life, a principle higher than reason, the impulse of the Holy Ghost, to fit harmoniously into the picture of man. "The gifts (of the Holy Ghost) surpass the ordinary perfection of the virtues, not as regards the kind of works . . . but as regards the manner of working, in respect of man being moved by a higher principle." [10] Viewed from this angle, the doctrine of the gifts is of supreme importance. We can understand now without further explanation why St. Thomas asserts that the gifts of the Holy Ghost are necessary for salvation. It is obvious, too, that the doctrine reproduces what is traditional teaching, and that it calls for the gifts as the Messianic graces of which Isaias speaks, requisite for achieving the plenitude of grace and the assimilation to Christ necessary for every Christian. The only difference from the older view is in the fact that the connection with Christ as the source of these gifts is not so evident.

The complete and precise significance revealed by Scholastic teaching on the gifts of the Holy Ghost may be expressed roughly as follows.

Over and above the ordinary Christian effort based on the virtues, there is a life controlled immediately by the Holy Ghost, leading, by means of the gift of wisdom, that is, in mystical contemplation, to an experiencing and tasting of the divine. The simple formulas which St. Thomas discovers for the contemplative life prove that, in treating of it, he is not thinking at all of special psychological experiences: he does not mention the immediate knowledge of God, which is thrust into such prominence today. The activity of the contemplative life, mystical contemplation—that this is the matter under discussion when

[10] *Summa*, Ia IIae, q.68, a.2 ad 1.

St. Thomas speaks of *contemplatio* is clear especially
from the parallelism with the teaching of St. Gregory
the Great—is based on the gifts of the Holy Ghost.
As such, it implies the plenitude of Christian life.
Therefore in mystical contemplation lies that Christian perfection which is itself to be realized in all the
redeemed, and through which they are assimilated
to the Redeemer in the highest degree. If, in connection with the doctrine of the gifts and with the questions on the contemplative life, St. Thomas makes
no explicit reference to the possibility of immediate
knowledge of God or to special happenings in the
soul, this omission does not imply that he failed altogether to recognize the mystical state as something
distinctive in the soul, or, at any rate, deemed it unworthy of a scientific investigation. We may conclude
merely that for him the mystical life is not bound up
essentially either with the immediate knowledge of
God or with special psychological occurrences. For
him the essential core of the mystical is not to be
conceived in purely psychological terms.

Of special significance for mysticism is the association of the gift of wisdom with supernatural charity.
By it a purely intellectualistic interpretation of Christian perfection is rendered impossible. The measure
of Christian perfection is the degree of charity. According to this latter also contemplation is graded.
The consummation of charity, therefore, ranks as

highest. That the gift of wisdom is claimed as the principle of contemplation, can be understood from the significance of *gnosis* (*sapientia*) in tradition. However, there is a certain difference from the traditional view in that, for the fathers, *gnosis* bestowed assimilation to God, deification, whereas St. Thomas resorts to, or rather presupposes, charity for that purpose, and that because he conceives wisdom, like faith, as being in itself purely intellectual. The fact that, in this matter, St. Thomas has recourse to charity, reveals a conscious effort to guard against an excessively intellectual concept of Christian life.

Thus the Thomistic doctrine of the gifts is rich in meaning, and is understood as being in accord with tradition, if we refrain from seeing its chief value in the mere classification and in the proof a real distinction between virtues and gifts. Its value consists much more in that it removes Christian activity and the essence of Christian perfection from the exclusive control of reason, submitting them to the direct influence of the Holy Ghost, who, especially by the gift of wisdom, in perfect charity, leads the way to a super-rational, mystical experience of the divine truth.

XI

THE GRACES OF THE CROSS

CHRIST has opened again to men the way to paradise; by sharing in His cross and passion, the faithful can return to their lost homeland. St. John Damascene makes this clear when he considers that the practice of facing the east at prayer expresses something more than a yearning for Paradise. According to him, by this turning eastward we fix our gaze on the countenance of our crucified Savior, who bowed His head toward the west.[1] This connection between a return to Paradise and participation in the sufferings of Christ is expressed also in the fact that, according to the opinion of antiquity, the chief inhabitants of paradise are the martyrs;[2] again by the fact that, in stories and legends, the tree of the cross is associated with the tree of Paradise. The way to

[1] *De fide orthodoxa*, IV, 12.

[2] "Si martyrium fecerimus, statim in paradisum, si paupertatis poenam sustinuerimus, statim in sinum Abrahae" (St. Jerome, *Hom. in Lucam*, XVI, 19–31). Cf. *Anecdota Maredsol.*, III, 385.

paradise lies, therefore, beneath the sign of the cross. We must endeavor to explain in greater detail the way participation in the sufferings of Christ (asceticism) is related to mystical ascent.

The relation of asceticism to mysticism can be explained variously. It is well known from the history of religions that even non-Christian, natural and demoniacal, mysticism demands asceticism. Very often this is constructed on a markedly dualistic basis. Corporeal life is reduced to the evil principle, the kingdom of evil; from this the soul, springing as it does from the divine world, must be delivered. It must set aside the body altogether—thus, more or less, Gnostic mysticism; Indian mysticism can, to some extent, be put on the same level, for even if, in this case, a single first principle is retained, the actual fact that the soul is chained to the body is traced to a fall from God prior to its existence in the world. In this opinion also the soul must be liberated from the prison of the body. Here asceticism is an actual deadening of corporeal life, an extinguishing of it apart from which the soul's full development is impossible. From this we acquire the valuable information that the idea of asceticism is associated with a particular estimate of the body. Our concern, consequently, will be to indicate the Christian attitude toward the body. Thus the nature of Christian asceticism and its relation to mysticism will be shown.

For the Christian the incarnation of the Son of God is the decisive factor in forming an estimate of corporeal life. Owing to it, an asceticism understood in a dualistic sense is ruled out. Were such a dualism supposed, God could never have entered upon so intimate and lasting a union with the flesh. Yet this is brought by Him to glorification. For dualistic asceticism the question arises: How does the soul come to be in the body, and what must it do in consequence to be set free from it again? In Christian asceticism the question to be answered is: Why did the Son of God assume human flesh, and what duty results from this for the mystic in regard to his bodily life?

Considered superficially, the incarnation could be interpreted as an unconditional approval of our corporeal being as it actually is. Appealing also to the Scholastic axiom, grace does not destroy nature, but perfects it, a person might be tempted to reject a Christian asceticism in the sense of mortification. Yet, from the Scholastic axiom nothing can be proved against some form of mortification. It is certainly not to be understood as though the Christian must give his approbation to nature just as it is. Its meaning is purely ontological, nor should it be twisted into a concrete, historical form. The order of grace, viewed in itself, is indeed the final perfection of man's being; but thereby the actually existing order of nature

which, according to the Christian view, is determined
once and for all, or better, is defaced, by original sin,
does not receive the approval of grace; it is not presupposed and further evolved by this latter simply as
it is. As far as the incarnation is concerned, we must
bear in mind that Christ, by His death upon the cross,
freed the human body from the confines of nature,
and that He has taken it up, transformed and glorified,
along with Him in His ascension to the right hand of
the Father. Thus the body of the incarnation and
nativity is not the final goal: it is glorified into the
body of the resurrection and the ascension. What
happened to Christ's body is by way of example in
our regard. Our corporeal life must be orientated by
what took place in the body of Christ from the incarnation until the ascension. In this process we must
estimate the glorification of Christ's body in its deeper
significance, in the context of the redemption as a
restoration and perfection of the state of the body in
paradise. Therefore Christian asceticism also must regard the corporeal life of Adam as its starting point
and, in a certain sense, as its final goal, side by side
with all that happened in the case of the corporeal
nature of Christ as the way to glorification.

Decisive for the corporeal life of Adam was the
perfect subordination of his body to his soul and of
his sensitive soul to the spirit. This double subordination served finally to direct his spirit toward God,

finding in this direction its meaning and foundation. We explained this when we spoke of Adam as the ideal of the mystic. With the divorce of the spirit from God because of sin, this line of unity in the spiritual life of man was lost. In place of this double subordination there entered in a disruptive tendency. Through the redemption accomplished by Jesus Christ this unity is to be restored. It is actualized in its highest degree in the human nature of Christ and, by means of sacramental union with Christ, its foundations are laid in germ in those who believe in Him. The mystic, who renews Adam's state of union with God in a higher measure than the simple Christian, must give clearer effect in himself to this double subordination. As it served contemplation in the primitive state, so will it conduct the mystic, too, to contemplation. Furthermore, since in Christ's redemptive work the path to a newly won relationship between soul and body traversed death, and since we must follow Him along this path to overcome the consequences of original sin, Christian asceticism is essentially mortification. Its aim is the death of human nature as corrupted by original sin, that from it a new human nature may be permitted to arise *in Christo*.

It behooves us now to define with greater accuracy the relation between asceticism and mysticism. Recent literature is almost unanimous in holding that asceticism and mysticism represent two distinct degrees in the spiritual life. Asceticism implies active, mysticism passive, perfection.[3] A further problem arises, "whether the distinction between asceticism and mysticism is one of degree or one of kind." [4] There are two conflicting opinions. The first requires for mysticism acts specifically distinct from those of asceticism. The second holds that the distinction concerns acts that are essentially the same, but that spring from a different efficient principle: in asceticism, from the human faculties assisted by the habits of the supernatural virtues; in mysticism, under the direct influence of the Holy Spirit.[5]

The distinction between asceticism and mysticism as two different spheres in the spiritual life presupposes the preponderantly psychological notion of mystical life rejected above. Certainly only with such a presupposition is it possible to conceive mysticism as the substance of all the supernatural states not explainable in terms of the ordinary powers of supernatural life. Thus it becomes imperative to look upon

[3] O. Zimmermann, *Lehrbuch der Aszetik*, 1932, pp. 1, 676. Tanquerey says: "We may thus define ascetical theology: that part of spiritual doctrine whose proper object is both the theory and the practice of Christian perfection, from its very beginnings up to the threshold of infused contemplation. . . . Mystical theology is that part of spiritual doctrine whose proper object is both the theory and the practice of the contemplative life, which begins with what is called the first night of the senses, described by St. John of the Cross, and the prayer of quiet, described by St. Theresa" (*The Spiritual Life*, 1932, p. 5).
[4] Mager, *Mystik*, p. 113.
[5] Saudreau, *L'état mystique*, 1921, pp. 147 f.

Christian life as the simple exercise of virtue, that is, as asceticism, until special psychological reactions make their appearance. If this exclusively psychological interpretation of mysticism is rejected, then asceticism must be regarded, not as a preparatory stage, but as one aspect of mystical life: the process of dying to the sinful life of the flesh. Asceticism and mysticism are the two factors of the supernatural vital process.

Origen expresses this view clearly when he says that neither πρᾶξις (asceticism) nor θεωρία (mysticism) can be alone.[6] It is true that by the βίος πρακτικός Origen understands not merely virtuous striving in the narrow sense, but the whole position of the ascetic within the Christian community and the obligation imposed upon him by that position. But precisely in this is revealed the marvelous unity in which Origen sees Christian life. In his twenty-seventh homily on the Book of Numbers his concept of the unity of asceticism and mysticism is to be seen when he describes the ascetic path as that leading upward, upon which Christ came down to us and which He has thrown open to us by His ascension.[7] It is the path which the soul must take in any case after its separation from the body.[8] These notions are familiar to us from the description of the entrance to mystical union. Origen

6 W. Völker, *Das Volkommenheitsideal des Origenes*, 1931, p. 145.
7 No. 3.
8 No. 2.

sees this unity expressed again in the words of Scripture according to which the Lord led the Israelites
out of Egypt "in the hand of Moses and Aaron."
Moses, the lawgiver, is the type of *gnosis;* Aaron, as
high priest, the type of oblation, of self-conquest.
Therefore *gnosis* and sacrificing self-conquest are
necessary for the exodus out of the Egypt of the
world. "Thus each of the two hands (that of Moses
and that of Aaron) is needed by those who are coming
out of Egypt, so that in them may be realized not
only perfection of faith and knowledge, but also of
deeds and works; yet these two are not two hands,
but only one hand." [9] A concrete illustration of the
unity of asceticism and mysticism is afforded, for
example, by the life of St. Fulgentius (d. 533). When
his mother learned that he had become a monk, she
went to the monastery, but the abbot would not allow her to see Fulgentius. Thereupon she set up a
loud weeping in front of the monastery, that her son
might hear her and return to her. "Even at this early
stage," comments his biographer, "he gave before all
a reliable proof of his future patience amid sufferings,
and, as though he were inebriated with divine grace,
it was as if he did not know that it was his mother." [10]
Here an ascetic act, by which the young monk over-

[9] No. 6.
[10] *Vita S. Fulgentii,* chap. 4.

came his temptation, is viewed at the same time as a mystical act: "sober drunkenness" is a notion typical of mystical life.[11]

St. Benedict's monastic rule also points out the unity of asceticism and mysticism. Benedict, who, on the testimony of his biographer St. Gregory, was himself a mystic and ecstatic, makes no mention in his rule of anything corresponding to modern ideas of an introduction to mystical prayer. But, in the seventh chapter on humility, he develops twelve degrees of asceticism which are intended to deliver the monk more and more from the purely natural life, and lead him to perfect charity. The enumeration of various degrees of humility is reminiscent of the degrees of mystical ascent. Furthermore, Benedict compares the ladder of humility to Jacob's ladder, a typically mystical image. At the end, after the twelve degrees, St. Benedict observes that, now the monk has climbed all these steps, he will soon reach perfect charity. Then he will practice monastic life, that is, ascetic life, as it were, naturally and without difficulty—a fact which the Holy Ghost will make manifest in him also. In this there must be admitted a direct allusion to that mystical life of grace which emerges, now that the life of the flesh has been mortified. A recent commentator on the holy rule is consequently quite justified in saying: "The seventh chapter on humility is

[11] H. Lewy, *Sobria ebrietas*, 1929.

for us the chapter on θεωρία in the old sense of the word, that is, on contemplation." [12]

Asceticism and mysticism appear clearly in their intrinsic connection in the explanation of the forty stations in the desert given by Origen in his homily on the Book of Numbers mentioned already. For Origen the basis of the spiritual life is belief in the incarnation of Christ. Then the ascent can begin.[13] The first stations describe the first steps: the break with the world, the recognition that man has no permanent dwelling on earth, struggle with the forces opposed to God, etc. After these first steps, the wanderer has to endure the most acute sufferings and trials. These never leave him now: he must bear them until he reaches the last and highest degree. But meanwhile the Lord bestows upon the soul consolations of many kinds, which strengthen it and brace it for the toils still to come. In these comforting visions diabolical temptations can also lie hidden, for even the devil appears sometimes as an angel of light. As the wandering continues, the visions increase, but later, in the higher degrees of perfection, they withdraw. On this point later mystical tradition is in full agreement; according to it ec-

[12] *Explication ascétique et historique de la règle de S. Benoît*, 1901, I, 270 f.

[13] "Et haec sit prima nobis mansio de Aegypto exire volentibus, in qua relicto idolorum cultu et daemoniorum, non deorum veneratione credimus Christum natum ex virgine et Spiritu Sancto et Verbum carnem factum venisse in hunc mundum. Post haec jam proficere et adscendere ad singulos quosque fidei et virtutum gradus nitamur" (no. 3).

stasies and visions grow rarer toward the end of the
path to mystical union. Occasionally Origen gives
an interpretation to the many persecutions to which
the wanderer is exposed. They are a particularly
strong incitement for the soul to guard against care-
lessness. "There are many encounters to be with-
stood; as in a wrestling match, there is a frequent up
and down; a single victory will not suffice." This,
too, Origen makes clear in connection with the wandering of the people of Israel in the desert. Only after
many struggles and trials of various kinds did the
numbering of the people take place.[14] On this occasion Origen points to St. Paul, who, in spite of his
sublime and extraordinary endowment of grace, had
nevertheless to feel the sting in his flesh.[15]

Thus asceticism and mysticism are not two sections
of one life canceling each other: they are bound together permanently. Here, too, the old distinction
forces itself upon us once more. Not every baptized
person is a mystic: but, since asceticism and mysticism form a unity, neither can every individual be an
ascetic, even if sometimes he puts into practice the
greatest amount of self-conquest to avoid a sin. In
such a case it is not a question of intensifying and increasing his supernatural life: rather he musters together all his strength to save his state of grace from

[14] Völker, *op. cit.*, p. 65.
[15] No. 12.

death. He is merely doing what is absolutely necessary to preserve his supernatural life. That is not the
attitude of a mystic; neither is it the attitude of an
ascetic.

From this unity of asceticism and mysticism there
follow important consequences for the understanding
of supernatural life, for the essence of our state of
grace.

The grace of Christ, the principle of our supernatural life, is different in its workings from the grace
of Adam, our first parent. The grace of Christ, unlike
that of Paradise, does not deliver us from suffering,
nor does it free us from internal and external difficulties, but renders all these things of service to the
unfolding of supernatural life. Even if, in the case of
a saint, this grace to some extent imitates the effects of
grace in the primitive state—so that sensuality dimin-
ishes, the saint exercises control over brute creation,
and his body withstands corruption—still the grace
of the original state will never be restored completely
in this world. In this matter we must not limit our
gaze to man. As the grace of Adam was related to the
external world-order (cf. the relation of the microcosm to the macrocosm), so also is the grace of Christ.

The Church, through which Christ's grace flows
down to us, is as yet neither paradise nor the consummated kingdom of heaven. But it bears within
itself the essential principle of both, supernatural

grace. It is each in a different guise. The Church, which as the body of Christ lives the life of the Lord, is in this world the crucified body of Christ. The grace which it bestows is the grace of the crucified One, a grace which ennobles and sanctifies suffering, but does not remove it.[16] Only in the consummation, when the Church has become the fully achieved kingdom of God, will the grace of Christ work a complete transformation of our corporeal being and renew the cosmos. Our graces are accordingly graces of the cross; through them the sinful man dies, the new, sanctified man is developed. In certain supreme manifestations of grace, man steps out of his corporeal being to unite himself to God without hindrance.

On the other hand, as was said above, in the highest stage of mystical life, when death has overspread the sinful flesh, ecstasies and visions almost cease. Thus it follows that psychological ecstasy does not belong to the essence of contemplation. In this too there is involved a manifest rejection of dualistic asceticism, and expression is given also to the nature of the grace of Christ: it is grace in the life of the Church, grace of the crucified body of the Lord, still waiting for its consummation and glorification and thus for the full assimilation to its Head, Jesus Christ. Only then does it bestow a life which no longer raises the soul

[16] Journet, "Les destinées du royaume de Dieu" in *Nova et Vetera,* 1935, pp. 71 ff.

out of its corporality, but elevates this latter and glorifies it.

From the standpoint of the corporality of human nature, not yet entirely redeemed, and in conjunction with what was said in the previous chapter about the essence of mystical experience, it is possible to provide an explanation also of the doctrine of the spiritual senses. Mystical literature mentions feeling and tasting God. In this matter Poulain bases his teaching on the soul's immediate contact with God. However much this latter assertion is to be accepted, the doctrine of the spiritual senses seems to have a different explanation theologically. It implies the redemption of sense-knowledge from the dulling effect consequent on original sin. Owing to the loss of original grace, sense-knowledge has to a certain extent been narrowed down to its proper object, whereas previously it played its part after its own fashion in the process of union between the spirit and God. The bliss of the spirit found an echo in it as well. In the paradisiac state the whole man rejoiced in intimate union with God. In mystical union with God we have an analogous occurrence. The spirit rejoices in intimate union with God. By means of asceticism the Holy Ghost, the efficient cause of mystical contemplation, regains control also over the other faculties of man, and they for their part are made aware of their share in mystical union with God. Thus we can

understand if mystics speak also of this experience
of God. We have here a happening which by its very
nature is remote from the sphere of psychological
analysis; and it cannot be satisfactorily recorded by
purely human means of expression. Modern mysticism, proceeding from a one-sided psychological
standpoint and frequently overlooking the theological foundations of mysticism, has sacrificed this doctrine of the spiritual senses. The latter asserts a
spiritualization, an activity of the senses under the
control of the Holy Ghost, not the presence of special
senses in the spirit in contrast to the senses of the animal soul. Mystical experience can also be attested externally in the life of the body. This is the significance
of many tokens which we read of in the lives of the
saints: heavenly light gleams forth; the scent of pre-
cious perfumes is wafted down; celestial music and
angelic choirs are heard. These are indications that
for the saint the life of the soul has been delivered
from the confines of its purely natural being and has
obtained a share in the spirit's union with God.

Something else, too, is to be learned from the intrinsic unity of asceticism and mysticism: the significance of martyrdom in the Christian ideal of holiness.

Poulain raises the question whether all the saints
have led a mystical life. He arrives at the view that in
actual fact all canonized saints have been endowed
by God with mystical grace also. In his inquiry he

excepts the martyrs.[17] He is able to exclude them from his inquiry only because, to his mind, mysticism and Christian perfection are not related to each other essentially: martyrdom, that is, sanctity, is conceivable without mysticism. Now it is certain that the Church regards the martyrs as the ideal of holiness. In her eyes, they are par excellence *the* saints.[18] Again, the martyr is undoubtedly the greatest ascetic, surrendering as he does his entire corporeal life for Christ's sake. If asceticism and mysticism are really one, and if mysticism is the highest development of Christian perfection, then the martyr must be a mystic. Martyrdom without mysticism is impossible. That martyrdom is not just asceticism, but also mysticism, is implied in the fact that in the martyr ecstasy is realized to its full extent. He steps completely out of this life to unite himself with God. Only a one-sided, psychological notion of mysticism could go so far as, not merely to separate asceticism from mysticism, but to fail altogether in recognizing as such the supreme embodiment of ecstasy, an embodiment which cannot be contained within the limits of a special psychological

[17] "Let us speak now of great sanctity, that which leads openly to canonization. Is it to be met with without the mystic graces? It will, of course, be understood that we must study it solely in the cases of those who were not martyrs and whose interior lives are known in some detail. For with regard to the martyrs, their death sufficed for their canonization without any heroic virtues having been previously exhibited" (Poulain, *op. cit.*, p. 523).

[18] Viller, "Martyre et perfection" in *Revue d'ascétique et de mystique*, 1925, pp. 3–25.

incident, since relation between body and soul has been completely suspended. In this, Poulain's purely psychological conception is reduced to absurdity.

The acts of the martyrs frequently refer to the martyrs' mystical state. Thus we read, for example, in the acts of SS. Perpetua and Felicitas: "And the two stood side by side, and the cruelty of the people being now appeased, they were recalled to the gate of life . . . and, being aroused from what seemed like sleep, so completely had Perpetua been in the spirit and in ecstasy, she began to look about her, and said to the amazement of all: 'When we are to be thrown to the heifer, I cannot tell.' When she heard what had already taken place, she refused to believe it till she had observed certain marks of ill-usage on her body and dress." [19] At the martyrdom of St. Carpus: "And Carpus being nailed after Papylus, smiled on them; and the bystanders were astonished and said to him: 'What made you laugh?' And the blessed one said: 'I saw the glory of the Lord, and I was glad, and at the same time I was rid of you, and have no part in your misdeeds.'" [20] The martyr, standing on the

[19] *Acts of the Early Martyrs.* Translation and notes by E. C. E. Owen, 1927, p. 91.

[20] *Ibid.,* p. 45. In the mysticism of the martyr there need be no question of happenings corresponding to the visions and psychological states of ecstasy here mentioned. Yet these accounts may be accepted as typical of that mystical experience of God always implied in the martyr's surrender of himself to God in perfect charity. It cannot be objected against this that a martyr with mere attrition can in no case be a mystic. Martyrdom without an act of perfect

threshold of time and eternity, already sees in his martyrdom the glory of the world to come, and is rendered thereby a "witness" to the glory of the Lord. Precisely on that account is he declared, in the estimation of the Church, to be the highest mystic. Holy Scripture testifies to this in the case of the first martyr, St. Stephen: "But he, being full of the Holy Ghost, looking up steadfastly to heaven, saw the glory of God and Jesus standing on the right hand of God. And he said: 'Behold, I see the heavens opened and the Son of man standing on the right hand of God' " (Acts 7:55). For the Church, therefore, the martyr is the saint par excellence: he is at once ascetic and mystic. He embodies the unity of asceticism and mysticism. Again we see proved true that mystical life is the full evolution of Christian being.

charity is, in the opinion of theologians, impossible. According to St. Thomas, martyrdom is "maximae charitatis signum" (*Summa*, IIa IIae, q.124, a.3). That later theology has held fast to this view is clear from Gonet, *Clypeus theol. thom. de baptismo et confirm.*, disp. 1, art. 7, no. 141.

XII

THE KINGDOM OF THE FATHER

THE mystical life is in a certain sense a restoration of the paradisiac union with God. On the other hand, the grace of Christ bestows something more than a mere recovery of the grace of the original state. Hence the mystical life cannot be explained in its entirety from the oneness with God enjoyed by Adam. It transcends this latter. Even now the mystic acquires part in the kingdom of heaven, the kingdom of the Father. Hence the final stage of contemplation is not infrequently described by mystical writers as *regnum Dei* and *regnum Patris*.[1] In the kingdom of the Father, the mystic experiences the special relationships to the individual Persons, in particular to the Father, upon which he has entered.

Jerome Jaegen, a mystic of recent date, speaks expressly of his relation to the three Persons: "The Holy Ghost prepares the soul for union with the

---

[1] Marsili, *Giovanni Cassiano ed Evagrio Pontico*, 1936, p. 107.

Savior and draws it ever nearer to Him in a mystical manner. The mediator and, at the same time, the spouse's guide to the heavenly Father is the Son of God. At the second stage . . . by slow degrees He raises His spouse aloft in spirit, ever higher above all the goods of this earth, and conducts her to the heavenly Father, so that He dwells with her in His presence even now here below." Jaegen also refers to the part taken by the three Persons in bringing about mystical union: "In the beginning of the mystical life it is principally the Holy Ghost with whom the soul has personal intercourse. He leads it to the Savior. Thereupon the Savior conducts it to the heavenly Father." [2] Significant, too, is his description of the relationship to the Father: "From now on the relations of the soul with the heavenly Father grow more childlike and confident. The soul feels how the eye of the heavenly Father is constantly resting on it in a paternal manner. It struggles with ever increasing determination to meet this paternal gaze, to bury its gaze more and more with childlike innocence in His. Thus it finds the Father. Henceforward it has as easy access to Him as it had hitherto to the Savior." [3]

This extract is characteristic of the experience of the mystics in the highest stage of union with God. From the relations to the Trinity, Scaramelli singles

[2] *Erlebnisse und Bekentnisse eines heiligmässigen Bankdirektors,* 1934, p. 190.
[3] *Ibid.*

out as a matter of the greatest importance and as an indispensable condition for the highest degree of mystical union, a vision of the Holy Trinity, and the awareness of its indwelling in the heart of the sanctified one; further, an apparition of the divine Word so that the so-called mystical marriage may be prepared for and entered upon.[4] It is clear from Scaramelli that in this highest degree there is question of two things, a knowledge of the three divine Persons, and a special union with the Word; in the Spirit the mystic attains to the Word, and through the Word to the Father. These two elements are now to be explained.

That a special knowledge of the triune God belongs essentially to the highest degree of mystical union can be elucidated from several angles; to begin with, from that of the connection between deification and the intellectual vision of God. For one who does not know God as He really is, there can be no question of a true deification. Every seeking after God must therefore end in the divine Trinity. This is given prominence in the *Proslogion* of St. Anselm, who seeks after God, and indeed first of all in the contem-

---

[4] J. B. Scaramelli, *Direttorio mistico*, 1754, tr. 3, cap. 24. Scaramelli, in keeping with his psychological conception, speaks only of extraordinary mystical phenomena. For us it is essential that at the end of the mystical life the Holy Trinity steps into the foreground, in particular the Second Person, with whom the soul, because of the incarnation, feels itself united in a special way. Accounts of a "marriage" with all three Persons appear as quite isolated and are obviously erroneous.

plation of the divine attributes and of the divine essence. But then he directs his gaze toward the three
Persons: "This good art Thou, God the Father; this
good is Thy Word, which is called the Son; . . . the
same good is the love common to Thee and to Thy
Son, that is, the Holy Ghost proceeding from both." [5]
The precise reason, however, why mystical life must
reach its climax in special relationships to the three
divine Persons is this: mystical life implies intimate
participation in the life of God. The life of the mystic must receive the divine life into itself and be
transformed by it. Thus the divine life, as it is in reality, as it unfolds itself independently of our conception of it, becomes the determining factor in the new
life of the soul. God is not a lifeless abstraction; He
is life, a life-stream overflowing from the First Person, the Father, to the Second, and from both to the
Holy Ghost. A participation in the divine life must
exhibit this dynamic process.

Accordingly the mystics have endeavored to steer
human thought by every route toward the contemplation of the Holy Trinity. Their purpose is served
first by the doctrine of the traces of the Trinity in
creatures (*vestigia Trinitatis*). From the visible creation alone we cannot of course arrive at a knowledge
of the Trinity, as we are able, for example, to attain
to that of the existence of the first cause and of the

[5] Chap. 23.

final end of creation. Nevertheless it is possible to indicate in things a triple aspect which can put our
thoughts on the lookout for the Trinity. St. Thomas
in his *Summa* (Ia, q. 45, a. 7) summarizes traditional
teaching on this point. He begins with the fact that
every effect reveals to some extent the efficient cause
on which it depends. But such information can be of
varying kinds. Sometimes it is quite general, merely
implying that a cause has been at work. St. Thomas
takes as an example the smoke indicating that a fire
is burning, but leading to no conclusion about the nature of fire. In such cases we speak only of a "trace."

If, on the other hand, the effect acquaints us in
some way with the essence of the cause, St. Thomas
speaks of a strictly representational likeness of the
cause.[6] An "image" of the Holy Trinity is not to be
found in irrational creation. Material things cannot
represent something that constitutes the essence of the
divine Persons: the intellective procession from the
Father and the spiration of the Spirit in love. But he
does admit a "trace" of the triune God. Every creature rests to some extent and is confined within its
proper existence. Thus it points to the Father, who
as fountainhead of the divine life rests in Himself
and proceeds from no other Person. In so far as a

6 "Aliquis autem effectus repraesentat causam, quantum ad simili-
tudinem formae ejus, sicut ignis generatus ignem generantem, et
statua Mercurii Mercurium; et haec est repraesentatio imaginis"
(*Summa*, Ia, q.45, a.7).

thing possesses its own essential determination and realizes an idea within itself, it points to the Son, who proceeds from the Father as "Word" and "Idea." The bearing of created beings toward one another or toward the Creator Himself points to the Spirit as personal love.

This doctrine of the traces of the Trinity naturally presupposes an awareness of the mystery; it does not imply that a man can rise through his knowledge of nature directly to the triune God. That would destroy the transcendence of the Christian concept of God. Strictly speaking, its value is purely pedagogical. It is intended to show how each and every thing reminds us of the triune God and is able to put our thoughts on the watch for Him. By means of the traces of the Trinity man does not therefore arrive at a knowledge of the mystery, much less at a real union with the Persons. Hence at this stage we cannot speak of special relations to the three divine Persons as long as man is merely intent on the traces of the triune God in creation.

In rational creatures, in man and in the angels, St. Thomas admits a real image of the Trinity. In knowing and willing, because of the production of an internal word and of love, they mirror exactly that which goes on in God and which determines the proper existence of the Persons. In this matter St. Thomas returns to ideas inherited from St. Augustine.

The trinity in the soul of man (spirit, knowledge, and love) is the image of the Trinity in God. Thus man in himself is by his nature an image of the Trinity (*Summa*, Ia, q. 93, a. 6). This image is impressed especially whenever man is actually knowing and loving, because then he is actually bringing forth word and love also. The image is not perfected in self-knowledge, as the parallelism with what happens in the inner life of God might cause one to surmise, but when knowledge and love have God as their object. Then the resemblance to the life of the Trinity is most pure, for now internal word and affective striving resemble in form the divine Persons. "This trinity of the mind is not on this account the image of God because the mind remembers itself and understands and loves itself; but because it can also remember, understand, and love Him by whom it was made. And in so doing it is made wise itself. But if it does not do so, even when it remembers, understands, and loves itself, then it is foolish." [7] The search for God in the Trinity of Persons on the part of St. Augustine and St. Thomas rests on the fact that God as the supreme spiritual nature can be discovered and apprehended only by way of knowledge. He who knows and loves God thereby impresses the image of the three Persons on his soul. In this way he perfects his own being (his

[7] St. Augustine, *Trinit.*, XIV, 12, no. 15.

likeness to God) and at the same time mounts ever higher in his knowledge of God. By progressing in the knowledge and love of God, he achieves a higher self-development and attains to a higher life in God: "For to have the fruition of God the Trinity, after whose image we are made, is indeed the fulness of our joy, than which there is no greater." [8]

Even in this doctrine, which has been called the "Trinitarian mysticism" of St. Augustine,[9] there lurks a certain incompleteness. It is based upon a picture of the three Persons pieced together from man's natural dispositions. Although thereby no claim is made that the Trinity is knowable from nature, even so, the transcendence of the idea of God is somewhat diminished.[10] Moreover, this aspect of the divine life pushes the characteristics of the individual Persons into the background. It does not show clearly how man enters upon a special relationship to Holy Ghost, Son, and Father. What is emphasized is rather that man becomes an image of that divine being which unfolds itself in the threefold personality. This is rooted in the entire Augustinian conception of the mystery of the Trinity. In St. Augustine the preponderant in-

[8] *Ibid.*, I, 8, no. 18.
[9] Schmaus, *Die psychologische Trinitätslehre des hl. Augustinus*, 1927, p. 297.
[10] If this knowing and loving God is understood as dependent on grace, resting on the supernatural virtues of faith and charity, the divine transcendence is safeguarded.

terest is in the essential unity of the Persons, not in their distinctiveness.[11] Consequently in his great work *De Trinitate* he begins with the essential unity in an endeavor to understand from that the trinity of Persons. He shows how the one fountainhead of being unfolds itself unto threefold life in the eternal utterance of the divine Word and in the love of Father and Son. The image of God in the human soul is viewed also from this angle. It implies in the first instance an assimilation to the unity of essence in God. Man becomes an image of the Trinity in so far as he mirrors within himself the unfolding of the divine life unto the triad of the Persons. In this is contained a conception, peculiar to Augustine, of the process by which man becomes the image of God. It is a conception differing considerably from the pre-Augustinian notion. Thus the Augustinian "trinitarian mysticism" has its own peculiar character. It could almost be styled "accidental trinitarian mysticism" since it is concerned with an assimilation primarily to that divine being, which only in second instance evolves itself unto the triple personality. On such a basis a life in the triune God in the strict sense in not realized so far, that is, no relationship to the individual Persons is shown to have been entered upon by man. Strictly speaking, such "trinitarian mysticism" can be verified

[11] In this respect St. Augustine adopts a view of the Trinity which "is more adapted to the West than to the East" (Schmaus, *op. cit.,* p. 12). It stands in marked contrast to Arian subordinationism.

even in a pagan, if he is thinking of God and loving Him. In that case a certain assimilation to the life of the Trinity is present, without it being necessary for the subject to have the slightest idea of the existence of the three Persons.

To arrive at the full meaning and precise content of life in God, we must revive the pre-Augustinian conception of the mystery of the Trinity. In contradistinction to Augustinian theology, this conception begins, not with the unity of essence, but with the different Persons. It does not speak of one God distinct in some way from the Persons. For the older theology, "God" implies quite concretely a divine Person; in fact, the Father. It does not regard the divine being by itself, but always and exclusively concrete Persons. The First Person is the uncaused source of all the divine being. He is incomprehensible and nameless. He contains all being in a manner surpassing understanding. He is the abyss, the eternal silence. Only in the Second Person does the divine being attain to a concrete self-representation. The incomprehensibility of the Father is concrete in the Son. The latter, as a true copy, presents the perfection of the Father. In Platonic language, He is the existence of the divine ideas, and therefore the exemplar of all created being. The Holy Ghost, as Third and last Person, is the power of God externally operative, apportioning the divine life to creatures, admitting them to a share in

the riches of that life. We cannot here undertake the
task of presenting in detail the various theological
conceptions of the mystery of the Trinity, and of
demonstrating to what extent they are justified or
how in particular the equality of nature on the part
of the three Persons is safeguarded in the pre-
Augustinian conception. At present we are concerned
only with the anthropological consequences.[12]

To the mind of pre-Augustinian theologians, the
perfection of the creature, in particular the supernatural life of man as a special kind of deification, is essentially an assimilation to a divine Person, to the Son,
the first image of God containing within Himself
the entire perfection of the Father. The office of the
Holy Ghost as dispenser of the divine life to creatures
is to seize hold of man and to mold within him the
image of the Son. The basis of the assimilation to the
Son is the incarnation. The sanctified man is physically incorporated into the mystical body of Christ.
This oneness with the Son can be termed—the expression comes from a recent exponent of the doctrine
of St. Irenaeus—"accidentally hypostatic." [13] The union takes place in the Spirit of holiness; the Spirit is
the last Person, who seizes hold of the creature and

[12] Schmaus gives a brief exposition of both views: *op. cit.*, pp. 10 ff.
[13] Gächter, S.J., "Unsere Einheit mit Christus nach dem hl. Irenaeus," in *Zeitschr. f. kath. Theologie*, Innsbruck, 1934, p. 531. Gächter, as a matter of fact, applies the expression to the believer's union
with the Holy Ghost. On unity with Christ, cf. *ibid.*, pp. 524–26.

incorporates him into the body of the Son, assimilat-
ing him to the Son and thus rendering him a son also.[14]
Now the sanctified man takes his stand within the
sphere of the divine life. By his alliance with the Son
he is conducted before the Father.[15] Those who have
received the Holy Ghost and bear Him within themselves are led to the Word, that is, to the Son. The
Son in His turn conducts them to the Father, and the
Father makes them sharers in immortality.[16] Then is
realized what Jaegen said of the relationship to the
Father: "The soul feels how the eye of the heavenly
Father is constantly resting on it in a paternal manner. It struggles with ever increasing determination to
meet this paternal gaze in order to bury its gaze more
and more with childlike innocence in His." [17]

In this view one can speak of a life in God in the
strict sense of the word. Here it is no longer a matter
merely of an asismilation of an intellectual or appetitive soul to the being of God, a being which unfolds
unto a threefold personality. Mystical union with

[14] "Per Spiritum imaginem et inscriptionem Patris et Filii accipi-
entes" (St. Irenaeus, *Adv. haer.*, III, xvii, 3).

[15] For the Son stands "before the face of the Father." According
to Dillersberger, the πρὸς τὸν Θεόν of the Prologue of St. John's Gospel, accurately translated, means "toward God" (opposite to, or
facing, God); therefore, looking Him in the face, speaking to Him
(*Der neue Gott*, 1935, p. 214).

[16] St. Irenaeus, *Epideixis*, I, 7. Cf. St. Cyril of Jerusalem, *Catech.*,
I, 6: "May Christ Himself, the great high priest, in recognition of
your good dispositions, present you all before the Father and say
to Him: Here I am and the children whom God has given me."

[17] Jaegen, *op. cit.*, p. 190.

God is seen in its entirety as essentially Trinitarian, that is, in its relationship to the divine Persons considered separately, and in its incorporation into the dynamic process of the divine life-stream. This explains why "Trinitarian mysticism" in the sense of Augustinian theology is, taken by itself, insufficient. It does not give expression to the actual relationship to the individual divine Persons which arises as the result of sanctification. Nevertheless it is only through this special relationship that life in God in the strict sense is effected; because its essence consists in the fact that, incorporated in the Holy Ghost to the Son, we are conducted by the Son before the Father. This goes back to all that was said of the sacraments, especially the Eucharist, in connection with union with Christ as the ultimate basis of mysticism. In the Eucharist there is achieved sacramentally the highest possible association with Christ, in the sense of a complete transformation of our sinful being into the glorified being of Christ. Oneness with Christ frees us from our sinful being. In sacramental mode Christ lifts those who are assimilated in form to Himself out of the confines of time and conducts them before the face of the Father in a manner corresponding to His own ascension into heaven.[18] Participation in the Eucharist gives the believer his personal "rapture" out of this world. At this stage he is led by the Son to the Father

[18] H. Keller, O.S.B., *Kirche als Kultusgemeinschaft*, p. 355.

in the region of the angels, and in union with the Son he is able to stand before the Father and address Him as Father: *Divina institutione formati audemus dicere; Pater noster.* The assimilation to the Son and the intimate union with Him which is perfected in the Eucharist sacramentally place him in Christ before the Father.

From these, two consequences in regard to mystical life result: true mysticism is always Trinitarian, that is, implies definite relations to the individual Persons. Union with God can be accomplished only as a union corresponding to what God is in reality. The mystic never enters into relation with the divine essence without at the same time entering into relation with the individual Persons. Neither can he stand over against the three divine Persons in a similar way. The true concept of God will not allow it. If the mystic wants to be one with God, he must enter into the fulness of the divine life. A relationship to God as a single divine essence, a disregard of the notes of the three Persons, a desire to transcend them, would destroy at once Trinitarian mysticism, the sole genuine and only possible form of mysticism. Nothing but illusion and self-deception would be left. For the same reason all true Christian mystics, although from a theological aspect coming from the most widely differing schools, have found the climax of the development of their mystical life in what they have unanimously understood as being a Trinitarian mysticism.[19]

Furthermore, true mysticism is always sacramental and thus is built on the liturgical life. By any other but the sacramental route it is not possible to be seized by the divine Spirit, incorporated into the body of Christ, and conducted to the Father out of one's own being, which has fallen away to sin and to the world.[20] Here, too, attention must be paid to the distinction between the simple believer and the perfect Christian, the mystic. The mere reception of the sacrament of the Eucharist is not sufficient for anyone to become a mystic and to experience special relationships to the divine Persons. In the mystic, sacramental grace comes into consciousness: it must, in the sense explained, pass over into experience. The entire life of the mystic, the intellectual life included, must be penetrated as fully as possible by the sacramental, Eucharistic event, and transformed by it. It must receive its determination from the incorporation in Christ and from the deliverance out of its own sinful corporality. When he has succeeded in maintaining in his whole life the connection with the Eucharist, in standing in Christ before the Father, in gaining an experience of this life, then is the Christian mystic perfect. Then, too, he

[19] For St Ignatius Loyola, cf. H. Rahner, "Die Mystik des hl. Ignatius und der Inhalt der Vision von La Storta" in *Zeitschrift f. Aszese u. Mystik,* 1935, pp. 202 ff.
[20] Cf. *supra,* pp. 46 ff.

walks in the presence of God. For walking in the presence of God does not imply in the first instance a mere thinking about God, but is to be understood primarily in an ontological sense, that is, as being permanently in Christ before the Father. It can be psychologically helpful to guard the thought of God's presence. But what is essential is to preserve inner, sacramental union with God, and to carry this into effect in every action.

At this stage the Christian fulfils also the requirement of unceasing prayer. The relationship between mysticism and prayer is such that mystical union with God constitutes precisely the essence of Christian prayer. He, therefore, who maintains a mystical oneness with God, continues always to pray as united to God; he prays unceasingly. This prayer need not be expressed in an endless vocal prayer or in uninterrupted meditation. This unceasing prayer is realized in the lasting, permanent union with Christ, who, as the Epistle to the Hebrews says, stands before the Father to intercede for us always (7:25).[21] This attitude can in its entirety manifest itself psychologically also in special activities on the soul's part, in psychological visions and ecstasies. Under certain conditions, or in correspondence with special designs on God's part, this will be the case. The essence of mystical life

[21] "Numquid eo tempore, quo dormio, orare possum? Meditatio ergo legis non in legendo est, sed in faciendo" (St. Jerome, *De ps.* 1. Cf. *Anecd. Maredsol.*, III, 4).

and Trinitarian mysticism does not consist in such activities; for the present this will remain hidden and remote from observation until, united in Christ at the consummation of things, we advance with Him before the Father, and Christ, fulfilling His office of Mediator, conducts everything back to the Father, before whom then all our being will course on unto eternity in praise, adoration, and thanksgiving.

XIII

CONCLUSION

TAKING as our starting point St. Paul's account of his rapture into paradise, we have touched upon all the leading questions in the theology of mysticism. In so doing, we have been able to find an answer to the disputed questions which are of commanding interest at the present day.

At the outset we renounced the attempt to furnish a complete essential definition of the mystical, contenting ourselves with the notional definition of mysticism as the experience of God, a definition generally accepted today and fully justified in its wider sense. After the preceding exposition, which follows closely the lines of ecclesiastical tradition, we can now define this notion with greater accuracy, and thus synthesize the results of our inquiry.

In no sense does mysticism evaporate into a sentimental experience of religious truth. Such experience, considered by itself, has nothing to do with mysticism.

An essential characteristic of the experience of God in mysticism is that it proceeds from intensified supernatural life. Of its nature, this experience lies beyond the frontiers of what may be discerned psychologically, and it is not necessarily bound up with a completely new, hitherto unknown psychological state. Mysticism is the experience of that process of being drawn into the stream of the divine life, a process which is accomplished in the sacraments, in the Eucharist especially. Only by abstracting from this quite definite experience associated with the concrete situation of the Christian in his relationship toward God, can we reach a concept of the mystical which, in virtue of its generality, admits of application both to Christian and to non-Christian mysticism.

This is to touch on a factor which has grown in a certain sense ominous in modern discussions about mysticism: the science of comparative religions. A science based on comparison can get to work only where possibilities of comparison exist. In this fact lurks a notable danger as far as Christianity is concerned. For, in Christianity, there lies always, beneath all the forms admitting of a comparison with something external, a hidden element. This is much more important than that which lends itself to comparison; often enough it alone gives to the latter the meaning and value proper to it, a meaning and value which a person approaching from outside merely for purposes of comparison easily overlooks. Moreover, non-Christian mysticism, that is, in religious life outside Christianity certain phenomena which manifest a similarity to phenomena of Christian mysticism, is something exclusively psychological. Mysticism outside Christianity lacks union with Christ and is thereby deprived of the basis of any sort of genuine mystical life. In its case there can be question only of psychological reactions to internal experiences of some kind or other. Consequently the student of comparative religions, if he is to compare Christian mysticism with non-Christian in any way, will regard the former purely in its psychological reactions and define its nature from that aspect. Thus there emerges an essential definition of mysticism, common certainly to Christian and non-Christian mysticism, but reproducing imperfectly only the meaning of the former. The fact that a person ought to begin with Christianity to reach a definition of Christian mysticism is disregarded. Only from Christian being can the correct attitude to non-Christian phenomena be acquired. It will then be seen that these latter are no more in harmony with the nature of Christian mysticism than, for example, non-Christian sacrifices are with the essence of the mass.

Only by beginning with the notion of Christian mysticism can anyone rightly understand the doctrine of tradition on mysticism. In this way alone will we avoid the error of simply striking off from the list of mystical writers great doctors of the spiritual life, such as St. Augustine, St. Gregory, and St. Thomas.

We can now determine what exactly is meant by a theology of mysticism. It does not purport to set forth how theological conceptions can be estimated for religious life; nor does it aim at showing how superrational knowledge and higher spiritual union with God are to be obtained. The theology of mysticism is that part of theology which undertakes to bring to light the higher form of Christian knowledge in its foundations, presenting it as it is, and explaining to what extent it is accompanied by special psychological phenomena. A distinction should be made between the theology of mysticism and mystical theology. The latter signifies the higher knowledge itself; the former, its theological explanation.

The more exact concept of mysticism allows further of a sharp line of demarcation between the object of theology and that of the psychology of mysticism. The theology of mysticism shows that psychological reactions of a specific sort do not necessarily belong to mystical life, and are not an absolute standard of inner mystical life. In the case of persons of particular psychological dispositions such reactions occur with regularity: they render such individuals capable of sharing in the grace of mystical experience. In the face of phenomena of this kind, an initial attitude of suspicion may rightly be adopted. Such suspicion is justified theologically, because it does not affect an essential element of mysticism and because, in the case of a notable transition from the mystical into the psychological, the greatest likelihood of self-deception and of imposture arises. An excessive estimate of psychological reactions conceals serious dangers: the mystic may entertain a preference for these unessential and extraordinary states, and may regard himself as a chosen instrument of God; even an inclination toward the occult is within the bounds of possibility.

Alongside what we are tempted to call this natural onset, these psychological reactions sometimes have a charismatic significance: God can determine them to that end as external signs for the attainment of definite purposes in the life of the Church. These special psychological reactions constitute the proper subject of the psychology of mysticism; theology can merely accept and emphasize the explanation of them. Precisely because psychology can introduce a definite regularity into the psychological reactions, it is indispensable in practical life and for the spiritual direction of such persons as share in these experiences, to distinguish true mysticism from false.

Evidently mysticism is built on the sacramental and therefore the liturgical life, and is thus bound up intrinsically with Christian life, of which it is the conscious intensification and perfection. Hence in mystical life we see more clearly what man is according to the

Christian notion: a wanderer from the Paradise of Adam to that of God. He is not lost between the two, cast off and looking for the way; Christ has pointed out to him the road to the homeland. Indeed he possesses even now, hidden within himself, the pledge of the glory destined for him in that homeland. This divine life within him renders him a "bearer of Christ" and enables him, now that he is dead to sin and has received Christ into himself, to recognize his prototype in Mary, the virgin Mother of God. He emulates Mary, the physical mother of our Lord; in so far as the divine nativity is accomplished in his soul, he acquires a spiritual share in her motherhood. Therefore he becomes in a higher sense an image of the Church; by the divine birth he is assimilated to the motherhood of the Church typified in Mary.

As the consummation of Christian being, mysticism is nothing extraordinary: it is not a second way to holiness along which only a few specially called may walk; it is the way that all should traverse. If the faithful do not succeed in intensifying their Christian being and their faith into an experience of the divine in this life, then they will have to remove all barriers in the place of purification after death, so as to prepare themselves there for union with God in the beatific vision. Thus we can answer the question whether we ought to conceive a longing for the gifts of mystical graces. If we mean such graces as manifest themselves externally, the answer must be in the negative. External graces (stigmatization, even special psychological experiences), since they do not belong to the essence of the mystical, are not designed for every Christian life. But what constitutes the essence of the mystical, the experience of the divine life, may be striven after by everyone. For how could we be forbidden to aim at the ideal of Christian perfection? If the Christian pays heed to divine inspiration, turns from the distractions of the external world to the divine life germinating within him, intensifies it into experience, then he has become a mystic and, lamenting and rejoicing at the same time, he will confess with St. Augustine: "Thou wert within, and I without. . . . Thou wert with me, but I was not with Thee. Those things kept me far from Thee, which, unless they were in Thee, were not. Thou didst call and cry aloud and force open my deafness. Thou didst gleam and shine, and dispel my blindness. Thou wert fragrant, and I drew in my breath and do pant for Thee. I have tasted and do hunger and thirst. Thou didst touch me, and I burn for Thy peace" (*Confessions*, X, 27).

INDEX

Abnormal phenomena, 35 f.
Acquired contemplation, 8
Act of faith, 175
Active life of mystics, 85
Adam
  Christ the second, 27, 39
  contemplation, 99
  experience of God by, 100
  faith of, 99
  freedom from lust, 90
  gift of immortality, 90
  gift of knowledge, 90, 96 f.
  grace of, 38
  grace of Christ and grace of,
    209
  ideal of human perfection, 89
  the image of God, 87 f.
  knowledge of God, 97-100,
    103 f.
  and mysticism, 87 ff.
  mystics' ideal, 27
  Paradise of; *see* Paradise
    (earthly)
  St. Irenaeus on death of, 91
  sleep of, 97
  son of God, 89
  state of happiness of, 89
  subordination of body to soul,
    201

Adam (*continued*)
  vision of God, 97
Ambrose, St., Paradise of Adam,
  18
Angels, knowledge of God, 103
Anselm, St.: ecstasy of, 17; *Proslogion*, 93, 137; on relation to
  the Trinity, 219; on the spiritual senses, 137
Antony (hermit), St., rapture of,
  69
Apatheia, 92, 95: recovery of,
  93
Apostolate, St. Paul's rapture
  and his, 82
Apprehension of God; *see*
  Knowledge
Aquinas, St. Thomas; *see* Thomas
Aristotelian philosophy, St.
  Thomas and, 142 ff.
Ascension, significance of the, 63,
  201
Ascent, as growth in perfection,
  111
Ascetical theology defined, 203
  note
Asceticism: an aspect of mysticism, 204; degrees of, 206;
  dualistic, 200; mortification

Asceticism (*continued*)
  and, 202; and mysticism,
  199 f., 203
Augustine, St.: on prayer in name
  of Christ, 114 f.; *De Trinitate,*
  224

Baptism: evolution of grace of,
  173; "in His death," 40; image
  of God restored by, 169;
  mysticism and, 49; and union
  with Christ, 45
Benedict, St.: degrees of asceticism, 206; vision of, 73 f.
"Birth, divine," 172
Blessedness, degrees of, 123
Bodies, saints' incorrupt, 92
Body, Christian attitude toward
  the, 200
Bride of Christ, Church as, 129

Cabasilas (Nicholas), *Life of
  Christ,* 49
Captivitas diaboli, 58
Carpus, St., ecstasy of, 214
Charity: contemplation rooted in,
  189; gift of wisdom and, 196;
  as measure of perfection, 196
Christ
  baptism and union with, 45
  Church as bride of, 129
  descent into hell, 62
  fellowship in resurrection of,
  42
  fellowship with, 39, 43
  following of, 39
  grace of Adam and grace of,
  209
  mysticism and union with, 46
  note
  need of resurrection of, 61
  prayer in union with, 114
  second Adam, 27, 39
  significance of ascension of, 63,
  201
  union with, 38 f.

Christian life, mysticism and ordinary, 8 f.
Christocentric mysticism, 43
Chrysostom, St.: on earthly Paradise, 22; on St. Paul's rapture,
  82
Church
  as bride of Christ, 129
  life of the, 210
  mystical life and authority of,
  83
  no genuine mysticism outside
  the, 83
  pre-Augustinian view of the,
  167
  relation of mystics to the, 72
  salvation outside the, 65 f.
Concupiscence, freedom from,
  92
Contemplation, 6 f., 8 (*see also*
  Prayer)
  acquired, 8
  by Adam, 99
  based on the gifts of the Holy
  Ghost, 196
  beginning of, 33
  defined, 7
  degrees of, 118 f., 130
  ecstasy and, 210
  as grave of the soul, 123 f.
  kinds of, 8
  knowledge in, 9
  love in, 9
  nature of, 176
  Richard of St. Victor on, 103
  note
  rooted in charity, 189
  St. Gregory on, 68, 111
  St. Thomas on, 13, 164
  of the Trinity, 219
Counsel, gift of the Holy Ghost,
  187
Creation, man's dominion over,
  88, 95
Cross: graces of the, 198 ff.; tree
  of Paradise and the, 198

Damascene, St. John; *see* John
De septem gradibus contemplationis, 116 f.
Death: as consequence of sin, 91; and original sin, 206
Degrees: of blessedness, 23; of contemplation, 118 f., 130; of prayer, 116 f.
Deification: through grace, 148; in mystery cults, 76
Descriptive method in study of mysticism, 2
Devil, dominion of the, 54 ff.: St. Thomas on, 59
Dionysius the Areopagite: on mysticism, 11; on prayer, 110
"Divine birth," 172
Divine nature, participation of the, 148 ff.
Dominion of the devil, 54 ff.: redemption a liberation from, 70; St. Thomas on, 59
Dorothy, St., *Septililium* by, 50
"Dress, theology of," 169 f.
Dualistic asceticism, 200
Duality of person, 75, 79 f., 83, 85 f.

East, praying while facing, 107, 198
Ebner (Margaret) on heaven and paradise, 24
Ecstasy
    and contemplation, 210
    in mystery cults, 76
    of St. Anselm, 17
    of St. Carpus, 214
    St. Gregory on, 126
    of St. Paul, 78 ff.
    of St. Perpetua and St. Felicitas, 214
    of St. Stephen, 215
    St. Teresa on, 67 note
    St. Thomas on, 14
    value of, 125
    while at prayer, 107 f.

Ecstatic union, 121
Eden; *see* Paradise
Elevatio mentis, 110 f.
End, man's final, 144
Eternal life, state of grace as beginning of, 153 ff.
Eucharist: and the mystical union, 49 f.; in mysticism, 228
Experience of God: Adam's, 100; in mystical life, 173
Experience, mystical; *see* Mystical experience
Experiencing the reality of God, 46
Experimental knowledge of God's presence, 6
Expiation of sin, 55
Extra ecclesiam nulla salus, 65 f.
Extraordinary phenomena, 35 f.

Faith: act of, 175; Adam's, 99; virtue of, 174
Father, God our, 112 f.
Fathers of the Church, 4
Fear of the Lord, gift of the Holy Ghost, 186
Felicitas, St., ecstasy of, 214
Fellowship with Christ, 39, 43
Fides scientifica, 177
Flight of the spirit, 121
Following of Christ, 39
Fortitude, gift of the Holy Ghost, 187
Forty stations in the desert, 207
Friendship with God through grace, 151
Fulgentius, St., ascetic act of, 205
Fulness of the Spirit; *see* Plenitude

Gardeil (O.P.), *La structure de l'âme et l'expérience mystique*, 3, 141
Garrigou-Lagrange (O.P.): *Chris-*

Garrigou-Lagrange (*continued*)
tian *Perfection and Contemplation*, 3, 9; definition of contemplation, 7; nature of mysticism, 8 f., 47; purgatory on earth, 31; theology of mysticism, 10; vocation to mystical life, 32 f.

Gertrude, St., prayer of petition, 114

Geuser, Marie Antoinette de, experience of, 84

Gifts of the Holy Ghost
contemplation based on, 196
counsel, 187
doctrine of, 188 f.
fear of the Lord, 186
fortitude, 187
knowledge, 185
necessity of, 195
piety, 187
St. Thomas on, 182
in Scholastic theology, 182 f.
seven, 185
supplementary to the virtues, 193 f.
understanding, 185
and virtues compared, 184
wisdom, 186

God
Adam the image of, 87 f.
Adam's experience of, 100
Adam's knowledge of, 97-100, 103 f.
angels' knowledge of, 103
experiencing the reality of, 46
experimental knowledge of, 6
image of, 175
immediate knowledge of, 137, 139, 156-60
immediate vision of, 29
man the image of, 168
man's final end, 144
mystical knowledge of, 136, 138 f.
mystical presence of, 38

God (*continued*)
omnipresence of, 37 f., 65
our Father, 112 f.
participation of nature of, 148 ff.
presence of, 141, 149 ff., 231
St. Paul's vision of, 135
union with, 143 f.
vision of, 97, 143 f., 155
vision of the divine essence of, 161

"Gospel of Prophecy" in Isaias, 191

Grace
of Adam, 38
Adam's endowments of, 89
of Christ and grace of Adam, 209
deification through, 148
essence of, 142 ff.
evolution of baptismal, 173
fact of, 145
friendship with God through, 151
habitual, 147
life of, 156
mystical, 171
need of, 145
pre-Augustinian doctrine of, 165, 171 f.
St. Thomas' doctrine of, 143 ff.
state of, 147, 153 ff., 166: as beginning of eternal life, 153 ff.

Graces of Interior Prayer, by A. Poulain, 2

Graces of the cross, 198 ff.

Gratia supponit naturam, 143

Grave, contemplation as a, 123 f.

Greek mystery cults, 76

Gregory the Great, St.
Adam's knowledge of God, 103
contemplation, 68, 111, 123 f.
on ecstasy, 126
mysticism, 28 f.
on rapture, 74 f.

Gregory the Great, St. (*cont'd*)
St. Peter and the prodigal son, 127
vision of St. Benedict, 73 f.
Gregory of Nyssa, St.: on mystical perfection, 172; on prayer, 112

Habit, reception of monastic, 170
"Hearing" and "seeing," 134 f.
Heaven, kingdom of, and the heavenly paradise, 23
Heaven, the third, 24 f.
Hell, Christ's descent into, 62
Hellenistic mysteries, 76 f.
Holy Ghost: divinity of the, 166; gifts of the, *see* Gifts
Honorius of Autun on location of earthly Paradise, 21

Ignatius Martyr, St., yearning for martyrdom, 52 note
Illumination, interior, 101
Image of God, 175: man the, 168
Immortality: Adam's gift of, 90; as union with God, 90
Impulses of the Spirit, 185
Incarnation: need of the, 55 f.; and our attitude to the body, 200; and redemption, 60
Incorrupt bodies of saints, 92
Indian mysticism, 65, 199
Ineffable union with God, 136
Institutiones theologicae mysticae by Schram, 123
Interior illumination, 101
Irenaeus, St.: on death of Adam, 91; on heaven and paradise, 23 note
Isidore, St.: inaccessibility of earthly Paradise, 30 note; Paradise of Adam, 18

Jaegen (Jerome), on relation to the Trinity, 216 f.

John Chrysostom, St.; *see* Chrysostom
John of the Cross, St., on mystical knowledge of God, 138
John Damascene, St.: on facing east at prayer, 198; on prayer, 110
John of St. Thomas, on presence of God, 151 f.
Joret (O.P.), *La contemplation mystique*, 3

Kingdom of the Father, 216 ff.
Kingdom of heaven, heavenly paradise and, 23
Knowledge
Adam's gift of, 90, 96 f.
gift of the Holy Ghost, 185
of God: Adam's, 97-100; angels', 103; immediate, 137, 139, 156-60; mystical, 136, 138 f.
of God's presence, experimental, 6
mystical, 6 f.
in mystical contemplation, 9
obscurity of mystical, 161

Lactantius on inaccessibility of earthly Paradise, 22 note
Ladder to paradise, 107 ff.
Life of Christ by Nicholas Cabasilas, 49
Life of grace, 156
Likeness to God; *see* Image
Liturgical prayer, private and, 111
Love in mystical contemplation, 9
Lust, Adam's freedom from, 90

Mager on mystical prayer, 33
Magisterium of the Church, extraordinary, 11
Man: dominion over creation, 95; God the final end of, 144; the image of God, 168; image of the Trinity, 224; lord of creation, 88; a microcosm, 94

"Mansions" of St. Teresa, 119
Marriage, mystical, 121 f., 128
Martyrdom, mysticism and, 212 f., 215
Methods in study of mysticism, 2 f.
Microcosm, man a, 94
Molinos on prayer, 113
Monastic habit, reception of, 170
Mortification, asceticism and, 202
Mystery religions, 76
Mystical contemplation, 6-8: knowledge in, 9; love in, 9; nature of, 176
Mystical experience, 53, 163 ff., 177 f.: psychological reactions, 163; psychological state in, 179; St. Paul's rapture, 163
Mystical grace, 171
Mystical knowledge, 6 f.: obscurity of, 161
Mystical knowledge of God, St. John of the Cross on, 138
Mystical life
    and authority of Church, 83
    as evolution of baptismal grace, 173
    experience of God in, 173
    and normal Christian perfection, 179 f.
    open to all, 238 f.
    psychological element in, 165
    stages in, 116 ff.
    vocation to, 32 f., 48
Mystical marriage, 121 f., 128
Mystical perfection, 172
Mystical prayer, ordinary prayer and, 33
Mystical presence of God, 38
Mystical state, 8
Mystical union, 31, 36: Eucharist and the, 49 f.
Mysticism
    Adam and, 87 ff.
    asceticism and, 199 f.
    asceticism an aspect of, 204

Mysticism (continued)
    and baptism, 49
    and the Christian ideal, 35
    Christocentric, 43
    essence of, 5, 7
    Eucharist in, 228
    immediate knowledge of God, 156-60
    Indian, 65, 199
    knowledge of God, 136, 139
    language of, 4
    martyrdom and, 212 f., 215
    mortification and, 203
    natural, 64, 70
    nature of, 8 f.: Garrigou-Lagrange on, 47
    non-Christian, 37, 235
    and ordinary Christian life, 8 f.
    and ordinary prayer, 5
    patristic theology of, 4
    prayer and, 130
    psychological aspect of, 10, 123, 131
    psychology of, 237
    rapture and essence of, 82 f.
    relation to the Church, 72
    revelations and, 6
    sacramental, 48 f., 230
    St. Gregory on, 28 f.
    Spanish, 122, 131
    stigmata and, 6
    study of: descriptive method, 2; psychological method, 3; speculative method, 3
    theocentric, 44
    theological study of, 2
    and theology, 1
    theology of, 4, 236: Garrigou-Lagrange, 10
    traditional notion of, 25 f.
    Trinitarian, 223, 229
    union with Christ, 46 note
    visions and, 6
    visions and essence of, 82 f.
    vocation to, 9
Mystics, active life of, 85

Natural mysticism, 64, 70
Nature, participation of the divine, 148 ff.
Non-Christian mysticism, 37, 235
Nuptials, mystical, 121 f., 128

Obscurity of mystical knowledge, 161
Omnipresence of God, 37 f., 65
Origen on asceticism and mysticism, 204
Original sin: *captivitas diaboli*, 58; consequences of, 89; death and, 61

Paradise: and kingdom of heaven, 23; ladder to, 107 ff.
Paradise (earthly), 18 ff.
   accessibility of, 22
   continued existence of, 18 ff.
   the cross and the tree of, 198
   inaccessibility of, 21 f., 29 f.
   inhabited, 22
   location of, 18 f., 107: Honorius of Autun on, 21
   and redemption, 58
   St. Chrysostom on, 22
   St. Isidore on inaccessibility of, 130 note
   St. Thomas on, 22
   Walafrid Strabo on, 20 f.
Patristic theology of mysticism, 4
Paul, St.
   duality of person, 79 f.
   ecstasies of, 78 ff.
   rapture of, 12 f., 26, 34 f., 54, 72, 78 f., 133 ff., 163: and apostolate of, 82; St. Chrysostom on, 82; St. Thomas on, 14 f.; into third heaven, 24 f.
   unutterable words heard by, 133 ff.
   vision of God, 135
Perfection: Adam the ideal of human, 89; charity as measure

Perfection (*continued*)
   of, 196; growth in, 111; kinds of Christian, 32; mystical, 172; spiritual, 199 f.
Perpetua, St., ecstasy of, 214
Person, duality of, 75, 79 f., 83, 85 f.
Peter, St., and prodigal son, 127
Piety, gift of the Holy Ghost, 187
Plenitude of the Spirit, 181 ff.
Poulain
   The Graces of Interior Prayer, 2
   immediate knowledge of God, 139
   mystical marriage, 128
   mysticism and ordinary Christian life, 8
   mysticism and ordinary prayer, 5
   nature of mysticism, 8
   prayer of quiet, 120
   sanctity and mysticism, 213 note
Prayer (*see also* Contemplation)
   through Christ, 113
   Christian, 110
   definition of, 110
   degrees of, 116 f.
   ecstasy while at, 107 f.
   effectiveness of, 114
   facing east in, 107
   forms of, 8
   and God's providence, 108 f.
   Molinos on, 113
   mysticism and, 130
   mysticism and ordinary, 5
   nature of, 112
   number of degrees of, 117 f.
   ordinary prayer and mystical, 33
   private and liturgical, 111
   pseudo-Dionysius on, 110
   of quiet, 120: Schram on, 123
   St. Augustine on, 114 f.
   St. Chrysostom on, 112
   by St. Gertrude, 114

Prayer (*continued*)
 St. Gregory of Nyssa on, 112
 St. John Damascene on, 110
 St. Teresa on, 112
 seven degrees of, 117
 the three ways, 118
 unceasing, 231
 of union, 121, 125
 in union with Christ, 114
Prayer states, 2
Presence of God, 141, 149 ff., 231:
  experimental knowledge of, 6
Primitive state, graces of the, 105
Prodigal son and St. Peter, St.
  Gregory on, 127
Proslogion by St. Anselm, 93
Providence, prayer and, 108 f.
Pseudo-Dionysius: on prayer,
  110; on mysticism, 11
Psychological aspect of mysti-
  cism, 10, 123, 131
Psychological element in mystical
  life, 165
Psychological method in study of
  mysticism, 3
Psychological state in mystical
  experience, 179
Psychology of mysticism, 237
Purgatory, 30, 34: on earth, 31
Purification, way of, 30

Quiet, prayer of, 120: Schram on,
  123

Rapture
 and essence of mysticism, 82 f.
 nature of, 25, 68
 of St. Antony, 69
 St. Chrysostom on St. Paul's, 82
 St. Gregory on, 74 f.
 of St. Paul, 12 f., 24 f., 26, 34 f.,
   54, 72, 78 f., 133 ff., 163: St.
   Thomas on, 14 f.
 St. Paul's apostolate and his, 82
 St. Teresa on, 67, 75
 St. Thomas on, 14 f., 68

Rapture (*continued*)
 Scholastics on, 14
Rebirth, 172
Redemption
 cosmic aspect of, 60 note
 earthly Paradise and, 58
 the incarnation and, 60
 liberation from dominion of the
   devil, 70
 man's unity restored by, 202
 nature of, 55-57
 physical theory of, 60 f., 63
Resurrection of Christ: fellowship in, 42; need of, 61
Revelations: mysticism and, 6;
  to St. Paul, 13
Richard of St. Victor on contemplation, 103 note
"Robe of holiness," 169

Sacramental mysticism, 230
Saints, incorrupt bodies of, 92
Salvation outside the Church,
  65 f.
Sanctifying grace, essence of,
  142 ff.
Saudreau on immediate knowl-
  edge of God, 160
Scala claustralium (*Scala para-
  disi*), 130
Scaramelli on vision of the Trin-
  ity, 218
Scholastics on rapture, 14
Schram: *Institutiones theologicae
  mysticae*, 123; on prayer of
  quiet, 123
"Seeing" and "hearing," 134 f.
Self-awareness, 156 f.
Self-knowledge of a pure spirit,
  157
Senses, spiritual, 137, 211
Septililium by St. Dorothy, 50
Sin
 death as consequence of, 91
 dominion of, 54 ff.
 expiation of, 55

Sin (*continued*)
original: *captivitas diaboli*, 58; consequences of, 89; death and, 61
Soul: knowledge of itself, 156 f.; as spouse of Christ, 129
Spanish mysticism, 122, 131; *see also* Teresa
Speculative method in study of mysticism, 3
Spirit: plenitude of the, 181 ff.; self-knowledge in a pure, 157
Spiritual marriage; *see* Mystical marriage
Spiritual perfection, 199 f.
Spiritual senses, 137, 211
Spouse; *see* Bride
State: of grace, 147, 153 ff.; mystical, 8
States of prayer, 2
Stephen, St., ecstasy of, 215
Stigmata, 44: mysticism and, 6
Stigmatics, number of, 44
Stigmatization, 44 f.
Strabo (Walafrid) on Paradise of Adam, 20 f.
La structure de l'âme et l'expérience mystique, 141
Suarez, on presence of God, 150 f.
Suffering for Christ, 42

Teresa, St.
degrees of contemplation, 118 f.
on ecstatic union, 121
"mansions," 119
on mystical marriage, 128
on prayer, 112
prayer of quiet, 120
on prayer of union, 121
on rapture, 67, 75
on the transforming union, 121 f.
Theocentric mysticism, 44
Theological view of immediate knowledge of God, 139 f.

Theology
ascetical, 203 note
gifts of the Holy Ghost in Scholastic, 182 f.
and mysticism, 1
of mysticism, 1, 4, 236: Garrigou-Lagrange, 10; patristic, 4
"Theology of dress," 169 f.
Theophylactus on paradise and kingdom of heaven, 23
Theoria, 13
Third heaven, 24 f.
Thomas Aquinas, St.
Adam's contemplation, 99
Adam's knowledge of God, 98-100
Adam's vision of God, 97
and Aristotelian philosophy, 142 ff.
Christ's descent into hell, 62
on contemplation, 13, 164
doctrine of grace, 143 ff.
dominion of the devil, 59
on ecstasy, 14
gifts of the Holy Ghost, 182
on image of Trinity, 221
inaccessibility of earthly Paradise, 22
the incarnation, 55 f.
location of Paradise of Adam, 18 f.
man's dominion over creation, 95 f.
our knowledge of God, 104
participation of the divine nature, 149
prayer and providence, 108 f.
presence of God, 150
on rapture, 14 f., 68
St. Paul's vision of God, 135
traces of the Trinity, 220
Transforming union, 121 f., 128; *see also* Mystical marriage
Tree of Paradise and tree of the cross, 198

Trinitarian mysticism, 223, 229
Trinity, the
contemplation of, 219
image of, 221
man an image of, 224
mystics' relation to, 216 f.
pre-Augustinian doctrine of, 225
St. Augustine on, 224
traces of, 220 f.
vision of, 218

Understanding, gift of the Holy Ghost, 185
Union
with Christ, 38 f.: baptism and, 45; mysticism and, 46 note; prayer in, 114
ecstatic, 121
with God, 143 f.: immortality as, 90
mystical, 31, 36
prayer of, 121, 125
sacramental, 47
transforming, 121 f., 128

Unutterable words, 133 ff.

Vasquez on presence of God, 150
Virtue of faith, 174
Virtues: and gifts of the Holy Ghost compared, 184; gifts of the Holy Ghost supplementary to the, 193 f.
Vision
of the divine essence, 161
of God, 97 f., 143 f., 155: immediate, 29; St. Paul's, 135
of St. Anthony, 69
of the Trinity, 218
Visions: and essence of mysticism, 82 f.; mysticism and, 6; of St. Paul, 13
Vocation to mystical life, 9, 32 f., 48

Walafrid Strabo on Paradise of Adam, 20 f.
Way of purification, 30
Wisdom: charity and gift of, 196; gift of the Holy Ghost, 186
Words, unutterable, 133 ff.